From BEDPANS
TO BOARDROOMS

KAY ANN HAMILTON

From Bedpans to Boardrooms
Copyright © 2021 by Kay Ann Hamilton

ISBN
978-1-956161-24-3 (Hardcover)
978-1-956161-23-6 (Paperback)
978-1-956161-22-9 (eBook)

TABLE OF CONTENTS

INTRODUCTION

My name is Johnny. Johnny Davis. I loved her from the beginning to the end. This is her story. It's a story that needs to be told to help others find their way. I think she'd introduce it by saying something like this:

> I didn't set out to be an RN, much less a hospital CEO, but what a ride it's been! This story is about that journey, written with the hope that it will inspire you to be all that you can be and, along the way, to bring you to both laughter and tears—maybe even at the same time.

CHAPTER 1

WOW! WHAT A NIGHT!

The surgical services waiting room of the small community hospital was packed with people, but not because of surgical cases. It was the meeting of the decade for this small town in south-central Ohio. The police were there, and there were guards at all the doors. Tension and anger permeated the room like sweat.

I saw the main members of the opposition group gathered in one area, laughing and bolstering each other. The board of directors and I were gathered at the front of the room, quietly maintaining a positive image. We were awaiting the final tally of the vote of the corporate membership, the vote that would either stop the impending merger of our small hospital with a large health-care system or approve it. It was, without a doubt, a watershed event.

My board chairman, Tom Baker, smiled as he said, "Well, Susan, this is what we've been working toward for almost two years. Finally we're going to see and experience the growth we need to survive."

There I was, at the front of this mob, and the cameras were rolling. Tom had called on me, as the president and CEO of our hospital, to give the count of the ballots. A hush came over the room as everyone waited to hear the outcome of this historic and volatile vote.

I leaned toward the microphones and said, "Mr. Chairman, I have three hundred twenty-five votes in favor of the merger and twenty-six opposed to the merger." At the same time, I thought, *We won! We won! My board and I prevailed!*

I heard a loud commotion and turned to see chairs overturning as a couple of men started swinging at each other. "Holy shit," I said as one of the board members, Jim, and a doc from the opposition group were duking it out right there.

Jim yelled, "I've had it with you!" as he threw a punch toward the doc, who ducked, spun around, and came up right in front of him, aiming to punch him right in the face. The doc sputtered, "You deserve this for what you've done to our hospital!" Within a couple of seconds, several other men had jumped up and pulled them apart. Emotions were heady, and everyone was nervous.

Suddenly, I heard a popping sound, and everyone started yelling. I felt a burning pain in my side, but I didn't know what had happened until I felt the warmth of the blood seeping from my body. "Oh God, Tom. I've been shot," I cried out. Then I thought, *Someone shot me! Oh, I can't die now—not after all we've been through.* I pressed my hand against my side as the world around me grew dim.

When I opened my eyes, I looked up at one of our surgeons, who said, "Good morning, and how do you feel?" I was very confused, because the last I remembered, it was evening. *What happened to the night?* I thought. Turns out, I had passed out and been through surgery to have a bullet removed from my side. The bullet didn't damage anything major, so I was very lucky there.

After all I'd been through in my life, I never thought I'd be shot then. That someone would shoot someone else over a vote on a hospital merger astounded me. But then I remembered the last two years, and it didn't seem so amazing after all. Those old-school independent docs were used to being in control and getting what they want. I could see why they would resent someone like me. But I didn't ever wish them badly. I actually understood and empathized with where they were, because medicine and health care were evolving into something that wasn't good for patients or providers. But shooting me wasn't going to change all that. I looked up to see my board chairman, Tom, smiling down at me. "We are so happy you're okay! Thank God it didn't do anything serious to you. But it's bad enough that you were even shot. I had my gun, but there wasn't any warning or anything, so I didn't get to shoot it."

This made me laugh despite everything. "Tom, it's hard for me to even acknowledge someone shot me over this merger. I am blown away by that and am glad his aim wasn't the best!"

Tom was also the local chief of police and was tall and fit. He had beautiful blue eyes, and we'd had a very special relationship over the past couple of years. I knew he always had my back. "Tom," I asked, "who was the shooter?"

"You could guess, Susan. It was your old nemesis, Howell. He's sitting it out in jail right now—no bail."

"Jeez, I can't believe even he would do something like this."

Switching topics, I asked my surgeon if I could go home. "Indeed you can," he said with a smile. I'll go tell them you're ready to get out of here." So, with a caravan of people and supplies, I headed for home—never happier to be there than right then. I had much to be grateful for. And we had to get busy and plan our next strategies. The merger had to be completed, and then the transition phase would start. *No rest ahead*, I thought, as I smiled to myself. *We accomplished the impossible!*

CHAPTER 2

NUNS AND WOLVES

It would be very hard to have had a worse childhood than I did. Over my whole life, I have jokingly (or maybe not so jokingly) referred to my childhood as being raised by nuns and wolves. This chapter is a part of my story that I don't really want to tell, because it's so dark. But not to tell it would diminish the rest of the story. Maybe it's a good idea to tell the story, because I'm not the only kid who had bad things done to her. This ugliness is all around us, and it might be perpetrated by someone you know: a friend, a neighbor. You just don't know—or maybe you do.

So here it is: Neither of my parents wanted another child; they were very poor and basically uneducated. They had children from both of their first marriages, and my mother had had a tubal ligation. But to their great dismay, she became pregnant with me in 1941. World War II was underway, and she was working as a riveter in an airplane factory in Baltimore, Maryland. She wore a staved corset so her boss wouldn't know she was pregnant, because she'd be fired.

She also had hardly anything to eat, so I was born weighing a little over two pounds. I was also a blue baby, so it was a miracle I lived, especially back then. My mother left me with relatives in Dayton, Ohio, where I went from one relative to another—anyone who would take me in. These relatives told me later that I was very tiny and usually dirty, with curly almost-black hair. My eyes were my distinctive feature. They are almond-shaped, and my pupils are almost black. People said they were sometimes even fiery looking.

Anyway, unknown to me, my father was hiding from the military, and my mother was doing whatever she was doing. So one of my mother's uncles took me in, and I lived with his family until age five. I have pleasant memories of my time there. But for reasons I'll never know, my mother came for me. She entered my life one morning, a strange woman who stomped into my uncle's house. She had dark hair and eyes, and she seemed very angry.

I ran to hide behind my aunt's long skirts, but this strange woman grabbed my arm and pulled me away from my aunt. I cried out, "No, no! Let me go," grabbing on to my aunt's skirts. Then this woman slapped me across my face and dragged me out to a car that was waiting there. I never saw or talked to my aunt or uncle again. That was the beginning of a really bad time for me.

Mom took me to Cleveland, Ohio, where my Irish father was living, working as a shipbuilder, having served a couple of years in the US Navy, where he saw combat. I remember clearly the first time I saw him. My mother and I had climbed a long, narrow enclosed staircase to a second-f loor apartment, and there he was, eating ice cream out of a cardboard container. I remember thinking how nice my dad looked with his black hair and hazel eyes. I wanted some ice cream, too, so I asked him for some. The next moments remain riveted in my mind all these years later. He took the box of ice cream and smashed it into my face. I can still feel the ice cream dripping from my face as I just stood there, tears mixing with the ice cream. My life in Cleveland had begun.

I went to the small elementary school at the neighborhood Catholic church. In retrospect, I'm not sure who paid for it, because my parents wouldn't have nor *could* they have done it. At any rate, I credit those nuns, even though I was scared to death of them, for the best education I could have received—an education that set the stage for my successes later on. They did smack me with a ruler or a yardstick whenever my Latin translations weren't perfect. Consequently, I learned my Latin very well. So, during the day, nuns governed my life. During the night, I was left to the wolves.

I loved the family who owned the house, the Bellinis. They were Italian and treated me great. They were a beacon of light in my dark world. I always got super anise cookies from them. The smell of those cookies brings tears to my eyes even today.

When I started to school, Angie Bellini always made sure I had food to take with me, and I stuffed it in my coat pockets. I still remember the aromas in her kitchen. "Mrs. Bellini," I'd call at her doorway almost every school day, and she'd appear, smiling at me. "Susan, are you hungry again?" she'd ask.

"Yes, I am, because I smell those wonderful cookies all the way upstairs."

Whenever I went there, they fed me. Just being there nurtured me. Mrs. Bellini would wash my hands and brush my hair sometimes, and I loved that. "Mrs. Bellini, if my parents go away, can I live with you?" I asked one day.

"Susan, nothing is going to happen to your parents, but if it does, we will look after you. You're part of the family." I was sad when we suddenly moved to another house. The new place was a two-family home with one side downstairs and the other side upstairs. We got the downstairs side, and it had a basement. The basement is where my tortures began. I don't remember what I did wrong but I was being punished for whatever it was. All I remember and will always remember is what happened to me in that cellar, night after night for several years.

My father, for whatever reason that provoked him, would take me down to the basement, spank me on the rear with a wooden board, and then do things to me much worse than a spanking. He would take my clothes off, feel me, and then tie me up naked and leave me in the basement all night. I spent far too many nights alone and naked in a basement with no lights. I had this old, tattered cover that could have been a blanket once. At least I had that.

I remember him saying, "now, Susan, this is for your own good" as he would pick me up and take me down the stairs. "What did I do, Daddy", I would cry, "what did I do? Please don't take me down there, please", I begged to no avail. I cried, I screamed, I even tried to scratch him but it was always the same. "It's for your own good, Susan.

You've been bad and you have to be punished so God will forgive you. You have to do penance for being bad".

I hated being naked and alone in that dark cellar and sobbed myself to sleep many times. I tried screaming over and over but no one ever came to even tell me to shut up. It was like I was alone in the world, a dark world. I finally gave up and, in reality, I acclimated to the cellar and to my plight.

He'd come down the stairs early in the morning. It was still dark, even outside. "Get up, Susan, he'd say as he grabbed me and pulled me out of my blanket. Then, he always held me up to him so he could stare into my eyes. "I know what you do", he'd say. "What, Daddy, what do I do"? I never got an answer.

This went on for the years that we lived at that house.

In retrospect, I realize that only by the grace of God did I survive mentally and physically. No one came for me when I cried. My mother never checked to see if I was in bed or not while I lay there in the dark night after night. I learned years later that my father and his two sisters were paranoid schizophrenics. That explained all the odd behaviors he had, such as putting microphones everywhere in the house and patrolling the outside perimeter of the house—not to mention the cellar activities. The really weird part is that I thought everyone lived like I did—until I finally got old enough to have a friend and see how others lived. I never spoke of my situation to anyone then.

During this awful time, one evening, I was actually in my own bedroom in my bed, and my half-sister (my mother's daughter, Betty) was there with me, along with my mother. They were very scared and said my father had a butcher knife and was going to kill them. They moved a dresser up against the door to stop him from coming into the room.

When he started pushing on the door, they jumped from the bed, opened the window, and started to crawl through it. Looking back at me, my mother said, "Susan, you stay here. He won't hurt you." And out the window they went.

My mind still sees the sheer curtains blowing in the breeze as the door to the room opened further and further. Then I saw my father with a huge butcher knife coming through the door. I sat on the bed and looked at him as he looked at the window and at me. I didn't make a sound, and he said nothing. Then I heard sirens, and soon there were policemen in the house, grabbing my father and putting handcuffs on him. I don't remember what happened next, but he came home in a few days, and life went on as usual, except my half-sister, Betty, returned to Dayton, where she lived with her father and brother.

Betty lived with us from time to time. I was about twelve then, and she was twelve or thirteen years older than me. I worshipped her. She was very pretty with her blond hair and blue eyes. She had a great figure and wore really neat clothes. I wanted to be just like her. However, my father hated her and made life miserable for all of us when she was around. That didn't stop me from following her like a puppy. I'd plead, "Sis, can I go with you today?"

"No, Susan, I'm going to work, and you can't go there." When she was gone, I entertained myself counting her shoes in her closet; she had thirty-nine pairs. I put them on and stumbled around in them, pretending to be her. I also wore some of her clothes and jewelry as I paraded around the house.

Late one night when I was all alone again and when I was around eleven years old, I heard a noise at the kitchen door – it was half glass. I went back to the kitchen to see what the noise was. I was very frightened when I saw someone at the door and he was rattling the doorknob. I could actually see this spooky-looking man and he was trying to get in! I was so scared that I ran around the house, trying to think what to do. Then, I thought, *Call the police!* I can still see the old black rotary phone in my mind as I dialed the number for the police. The funny thing is that after I called the police, I crawled under an area rug we had! I guess I thought if I couldn't see him, he couldn't see me.

Anyway, just as he got in the house, the police arrived and they got him! It turned out that he was an escapee from a nearly mental institution. I was saved! My mother was furious with me because she got in trouble with the police for leaving me alone at night.

Another exciting event occurred when I was around eleven years old. I was excommunicated from the Catholic Church (not formally) and thrown out of the Catholic School. You may wonder how that could happen. Well, it was easy. I was a prolific reader at a young age, and the nuns found me reading a biography of Martin Luther. You would have thought I had the latest edition of *Penthouse* for all the cacophony that erupted over that little book.

I was dragged to see the parish priest, who told me I would surely burn in hell for reading such heretical material. Looking down his nose at me, he said, "Tell me you are sorry and that you will never do anything like this again. And give me that book!"

"Father," I replied. "I won't give you the book, and I am going to read it. Besides, I can't imagine God saying what you said. God's not like that"—as if I knew anything about God. The priest told me to leave school and the church and not to come back unless I repented. Well, I never did. And guess where I went to church from there? You got it—the Lutheran Church.

I had to enroll in public school, and my father was furious. My mother, being the Catholic-hater that she was, smiled—a rare occurrence. So I ended up being baptized and confirmed in both the Catholic Church and the Lutheran Church. I think it may have helped in the long run.

I was an extremely homely girl—skin and bones with glasses and a long nose. My peers used to ask me to turn sideways and stick out my tongue so I'd look like a zipper, and they called me Zipper. I had terrible eczema on my hands and feet. On the public bus one day, a woman asked if I had leprosy. Honestly, why would any grown person say something like that to a kid? It was devastating to me then, and obviously I still remember it. But I did have what people described as exotic eyes, which they couldn't even see unless I took my coke-bottle glasses off.

I was chased by gangs of kids and learned how to fight at an early age so I could defend myself when and if they caught me—which they ultimately did. Strangely enough, I learned to fight by watching my Irish father in the fistfights he got into every week outside some Irish pub in Cleveland. Dad used to take me into the pub on

Twenty-Sixth Street when I was five and six and had me dance to Irish songs. I still remember the warmth I felt when the crowd applauded and threw coins on the floor around me. Dad had more money then to spend on beer.

Once we were outside, going to the car, Dad would get into a fight with someone. I watched how he handled himself, and though he wasn't a big man, he almost always won fights. What I learned came in handy for the scraps I got into on the streets. Despite what I learned or how fast I ran, my nose was broken at least a couple times before I was fifteen.

Here's a funny one: I was in the eighth grade, wore thick glasses, and had my nickname, Zipper. One night my mother decides to give me a Lilt home permanent to control my curly, unruly dark-brown hair. Now, being a child of the Depression, she left the solution in longer in order to get her money's worth. Well, when those curlers came out, I became the first white person in the United States with an Afro. Picture a zipper with this giant dark-brown head bobbing around on the top of it.

"Oh, off! Shave it off," I begged to no avail. I think she did feel bad for me, but I had to go to school like that—and I was in the eighth grade. You know how kids are in the eighth grade? They were merciless as they howled with laughter. Frankly, I couldn't blame them. I mean, even my teachers laughed. They tried to hold it in but just couldn't pull it off. That was one of my worst memories, for sure.

One of the things that saved me from complete self-destruction in childhood is that I became a distance runner and swimmer. I didn't know it then, but those two things were my salvation in many ways. I became a strong athlete; I gained confidence in myself; and I vented my anger and grief in those physical things. I think it saved me mentally.

Running was my real passion. I ran miles every single day of my life and swam in Lake Erie every day in the summer and the YMCA pool in the winter. I had a great coach who saw an athlete in me and spent more time with me than he would have otherwise. The bottom line is that I became an efficient running machine, and I loved the runner's high. Consequently, for most of my life, I ran no matter what: bad weather, kids, husbands—I ran. Swimming went by the wayside as I got older, because I often had no place to swim—a prerequisite for swimming!

Still, there was another ray of light in the darkness of my youth. I loved to dance—and it was the era of rock and roll. When I was in the ninth grade, a hunk of a guy, a hood named Johnny Davis, asked me to jitterbug. It was my first dance with a guy.

Johnny was a heartbreaker—tall, built just right, with wavy black hair and a lock of hair curling down over his forehead. Of course, he wore a black leather jacket to go with his tight jeans. I don't know what he saw in me, except that I could jitterbug like crazy, and he was looking for a good partner so he could get on *American* Bandstand and win. Well, I was his ticket.

"Johnny, will we win, do you think?" I asked him one night after we had been practicing for hours.

"With you, Chicky, we will win." He smiled as he stroked my face.

"Quit that, Johnny. It tickles. Let's go through our number one more time."

We had it down perfectly, and the way Johnny twirled me around his waist and threw me up over his head and down through his legs was powerful and sexy. He did it with such ease, but then I only weighed eighty-eight pounds, so I was the perfect person to be his partner. He was six two and I was five four. For contests, I wore a poodle skirt, a button-down sweater (on backward), tons of crinolines under my skirt, and of course saddle shoes. We literally danced many nights away. We were always the last dancers on the floor and often the stars of the show. "Rock Around the Clock" was our favorite number to perform and our best.

We had dance marathons where we danced all night long, nonstop. Potty breaks and water breaks were it! No wonder, between running and dancing, I weighed only eighty-eight pounds and ate like a friend. The best, though, was yet to come.

"Chicky," Johnny asked, "it's time for us to go to *American Bandstand*. It's not that far to Philly. Let's do it. We're ready." For sure, Johnny's dance moves showed his distinctive grace and flair. We weren't an item, Johnny and me, but he was a hunk—a dancing hunk!

So, off to *American Bandstand* we went. And you know what, we did win, though not the first time. It was so much fun just being there and seeing people like Dick Clark. We got to dance with people from all over the country with big numbers on our back for the judges to use in their scoring. In the end, Johnny and I won twice. I've always been proud of that and secretly imagined I could be a famous dancer.

I was around thirteen when we moved to another house, the house with the attic. Things changed then between my father and me. The basement there was very small, and my mother did the laundry down there, so my father continued my punishments in the attic and in a different way. Now he tied my wrists to some boards in the top of attic and left me hanging like that with my feet dangling for hours at a time. My wrists are deformed as a result of those nights.

Being older and a teenager, I fought back now but he was much stronger. I know I scratched him and I know I landed a few blows but nothing I did stopped him.

I yelled "Dad, what's this about? I didn't do anything! I'm going to call the police, I threatened but all he ever did was to look me directly in the eyes and say "I know what you do and you have to pay". I know now how wrong this was and that my father was just crazy but then, I wasn't sure about anything. I just didn't know how to get out of this mess. I was overcome by intense anger at him for doing this and at her for never rescuing me.

Most of all, though, I began to create my own world in my mind. I spent hours and hours fantasizing about this world where I would be safe and happy and where people would love me and there would be no more punishments.

I remember looking out the attic window, wondering if anyone would ever save me. I never thought about running away, because I had figured out that getting through school was my only real chance of getting out on my own successfully. I loved school, and I was academically very strong. I had an ear for languages and began studying French, Latin, Spanish, and Russian. I excelled in all of them and wanted nothing except a career interpreting Russian at the United Nations. These are the things that I thought about in the cellar and in the attic. In my mind, I created a whole new world for myself, much like I read that the survivors of the Nazi death camps did.

What really hurt me was that, never, not once, did my mother look for me or ask me about anything. She was gone most of the time, working two jobs and doing whatever she was doing. I seldom saw her and never really talked with her. Not until she was close to her death did she say anything positive to me.

She always talked about her two other children, who were in Dayton with their father, and how wonderful they were and how much she loved them. She said they were plump, beautiful babies when they were born, but I looked like a little skinny rat. That hurt me worse than the beatings, the attic, and all the rest that followed.

My father was crazy, but my mother was obsessive compulsive beyond imagination. She made me scrub (that's different from wash) the bathroom and the kitchen daily— including the walls and the floor. Yes, daily! She scrubbed them, too, mainly to supervise me. Once I didn't wash the dishes very well, and she found a plate with a smear of food still on it. I had to wash every dish in the cupboards that night, dry them, and put them away. I can tell you that I never had another dirty dish.

Then my family moved again, this time to a house that Dad was renovating. I call it the knotty pine house. The beatings and the other tortures stopped. I don't know why, but in their place came sexual advances. My father would tell me we were going to play a game, and I had to get in bed to play the game. I hated myself for years because I "let" him do those things. The games went on for two or three years. For whatever reasons (my athleticism or the torture), I didn't develop like the other girls, and my period didn't start until I was almost eighteen.

What he did to me now was so demeaning and yet, in a deep down, dark way, I liked this kind of attention from my father. It sure beat the cellar and the attic! I knew it was wrong but I did nothing to stop it. I didn't fight with him anymore.

My childhood, if I ever really had one, ended when I was fifteen years old. I had made friends with an Italian girl named Antonia when I was around ten I practically lived at her house, and were always together. Her brothers were great, and her family thought of me as one of their own. I knew by then that my family was not normal, though I never, never talked about them—not even with Antonia.

I also had my first teenage crush – my first puppy love for a teacher in my school. I met him when I was fourteen, and he was very good-looking with wavy light-brown hair and dark-brown eyes. But it was his charming smile that I loved and the mannerisms he had that I treasured and knew by heart. I lived for the moments we had together to talk about life.

He loved me, too—I knew it—but like a daughter. He was very professional and so very kind to me. I think he knew that I was abused, although I never spoke of it. He certainly recognized I was a troubled child, and his wise counsel has guided me all my life.

Anyway, one day, right after school started for ninth grade, a horrible thing happened. My best friend, Antonia, and I were at our lockers for our first year in high school.

I can't remember exactly what she said to me, but I know it was about this teacher that I loved—and it was hateful, like teenage girls can be. The next moments of my life remain a blur, but I clearly remember blood being everywhere—her blood. I had grabbed her by her long, blond hair and beat her head against the metal lockers. She was unconscious, yet I still beat her as people tried to pull me off of her. The dam had opened, and years of violence had spewed out—and I couldn't stop.

Finally, they pulled me off of her, and the police handcuffed me and put me in the squad car. Cuffed and stuffed at age fifteen! Antonia's parents did not press charges; it isn't the Italian way. Antonia was in a coma for weeks and was not able to go to school for that whole year. I didn't know it until years later, but she never walked again and spent her life in a wheelchair because of me.

I waited day after day for her brothers to come for me, but they never did. The only good thing that came out of it was that from that day forward, no one messed with me again. I had been beaten many times by other kids, but now they left me alone. I was a loner, but my languages, running and swimming, and dancing with Johnny were what I lived for—plus my dreams of another world where none of my agony existed.

By that time, I spoke four languages pretty fluently— French, Russian, Spanish, and Latin. Yes, Latin. I had four years of Latin in school—the first two of which were taught by nuns. I was so scared of those nuns, I wouldn't do anything else in the evenings until my Latin translations were done. The really weird thing is that so much of it stuck in my brain. I can still conjugate in Latin: *amo, amas, amat, amamus, amas, amant.* And I can still quote the first line of Cicero: "*Omnia Gallia divisa est in partes tres!*" All these years later, Latin still helps me. Can't find many people today who know anything about Latin.

At graduation, when I was honored for my academic status, the principal asked for my parents to stand. They weren't there, so when a couple stood, I didn't know what to make of it. Then I realized it was Antonia's mother and father, standing for me in spite of what I had done to their daughter. I felt a knifelike pain in my gut as I stood there. Many years later, on the one trip I made to a high school reunion, I learned why her brothers never came for me. Antonia's father had told the family that there would be no retribution against me because I already lived in my own hell. How right he was.

People always wonder why other people stick it out in an abusive situation. I can tell you why. It's many things. If you're a small child, like I was, you think it's how everyone lives—until you get old enough to know better, which I did at around eight years of age. Before that, I thought everyone lived in a cellar at night, and everyone had microphones hidden throughout their house. After that, it's guilt and shame that keep you from doing anything about it. You're ashamed of what happened (as though it was your idea), and you feel guilty because you let it happen without telling anyone. Then, as you get older (fourteen or fifteen), you experience more guilt because then you *know* you should have told somebody. Then you begin to realize that one of the reasons you didn't tell anyone is because you didn't want your father to go away.

There is also an element of recognizing that if you just ran away, life could be much worse, because you'd have no food and no place to live. For me, it was even more than that, because I knew that the one thing I had going for me was my education, and I couldn't let that be affected by running away. As it turned out, years later, I was right. The excellent secondary education I received positioned me well for the opportunities that would come my way later.

I was a real dork in high school. Academics and athletics were all that mattered to me. I never dated, was never asked for a date, and just thought that's how life would be for me. I had come to like the Lutheran church my mother and I attended. The minister was an excellent role model, and his son was cute and in my class. Of course, he never looked my way.

I had no real friends except Johnny. Johnny and I were close, and although we had no classes together, we still danced every weekend. "Chicky, your eyes are so different and dark, but I like it when they flash like lightning in the night," he said as we practiced our moves one night.

Ignoring his comment, I cried, "Oh, Johnny, I'm so worried about college. What will I do if I can't go?"

"Chicky"—Johnny's soft voice caressed my ear—"you need to relax. You scare people."

"Johnny, I'm scared not scary. I'm scared! I'm a kid and I'm scared. What's going to happen to me?"

"Oh, Chicky, why don't you just want to be some guy's wife and have a couple of kids. What's wrong with that?"

"Johnny, I thought you understood me. I thought you knew me like no one else knew me," I yelled as I whirled away from him and ran down the stairs. I didn't see Johnny again for a long time.

I had planned on attending a Lutheran college when I graduated from high school. I wanted to major in languages so I could be a simultaneous interpreter in the United Nations. I had saved several hundred dollars from my part- time work in high school, and I had a scholarship as well. However, I didn't understand that the college I chose was expensive. If I had gone to the closest state school, I may have been able to complete my education. But I picked a good private school, got accepted, and won a couple of small scholarships.

My parents had told me early on that they had no money for me. So I made it through most of the first semester before I realized I didn't have enough money, even with my job at the candy store. Those were the days before federal loan programs, etc. To go to college, you either had to have the money or be really good with a football. So I went to the dean of the college, thinking he might know of a job I could get besides the one I already had.

And you know what? He did. He told me I could make enough money for college and more—*if* I worked at a place he knew of that liked young girls. I was very slow on the uptake and didn't realize he meant being a prostitute. When the light came on, I grabbed my stuff and flew out of there. That was a devastating experience for me and pushed me away from God even more than I had been. "Why me?" I yelled at God. "Why did you do all this stuff to me?"

CHAPTER 3

OFF WE GO INTO THE WILD BLUE YONDER

When I joined the US Air Force at age eighteen, I had no idea what an impact it would have on the rest of my life. I was just trying to find a place to live. Obviously, going home wasn't an option, and I had nowhere else to go. I was mesmerized by planes, so the Air Force it was. And I thought it might be a place where I could further my career goals—translating Russian. Can you even imagine a more clueless thought than that? Only an eighteen-year-old!

A really interesting thing happened to me before I even got into the air force. While I was having my medical evaluation, several of the doctors gathered around my exam table, looking at me with a mixture of strange expressions. One of them asked me if I was born in the Orient. I said, "No, as far as I know I was born in Baltimore."

They told me something was amiss in my exam: I had almond-shaped eyes with almost-black pupils, and I had an epicanthal fold at the inner corners of both eyes. All of that indicates oriental or Native American ancestry.

Well, as soon as I was out of there, I called my mother. "Mom, what's the deal?" I said to her, telling her what I had just learned. Long story short, my maternal grandmother had a one-night stand with a full-blood Apache from an Indian School in nearby Pennsylvania. My mother was the result of that night, and then there was me. Can you even believe it? Of course, I would have loved having the scholarships I could have gotten if I had known this at that time and had a tribal number or even a name to give to someone. Today I value my ancestry in spite of how it all came to pass.

Arriving for basic training in the dead of the night after several hours in the air in an old troop plane and being literally dumped out on the tarmac at Lackland Air Force Base was intense. Suddenly I found myself in a foreign world where I was a commodity—and not a very valuable one. Wait a minute, though. Looking back from there, that feeling had a familiar ring.

"All right, you maggots, line up!" shouted—and I mean shouted, like the ground shook—a huge man I later learned was the infamous drill instuctor (DI). These people were there to drive me straight into the ground and then resurrect some new person, one that did everything the Air Force way. I had to pee—and that's all I could think of, I had to go so badly. Of course, being straight out of high school, I raised my hand and asked to go to the bathroom. Wow, what a mistake that was! The DI was on top of me, literally, in a nanosecond. "What, maggot?! You think the Air Force cares that you have to piss. Shut up and deal with it!" he thundered. At that point, it didn't matter anymore, because he scared me so badly I just peed on the ground. Problem solved. Plus, it was so hot, my pants dried before I got to sit down.

There's no way to describe military boot camp. You have to be there. I was in excellent physical shape and knew my left foot from my right foot, so I got along pretty well. I can't say the same for my peers. They suffered much more than I did.

After the first two weeks, in which I was miserable and depressed, I got really angry at our flight DI, a different guy. (Yes, we had a male DI for our female flight.) He probably weighed 110 pounds soaking wet, but he drove me to the brink of sheer violence every day with his harpy, nagging berating of me and everyone else. He wasn't very big, but he inspired fear by just looking at you. He was ramrod straight with piercing hawk-like eyes that missed nothing. To this day, I don't know the color of his hair, because it was so short I couldn't tell. He barked orders just to hear himself talk and kept us all homicidal. He'd say, "Troop, pick that up off the floor"—he had dropped it there—"light my cigarette"— lying right next to his hand—and any other absurd orders with a smirk on his face that I still remember.

We were marched all over the parade grounds until we thought we were in hell—in the heat, in the rain, or whatever. The huge worms that came out when it rained were a problem for me. I couldn't stand the squishing sound they made when my boots hit them (heels first), so

I tried to step around them. That didn't work, and after being screamed at, I had to step on them. Yuck! I hated that.

We stood at attention in the hot Texas sun for hours. The worst of that was the flies that crawled on our faces, in our noses, and in our ears, and the sweat we couldn't wipe away. Troop after troop fell to the ground and were carted away on a stretcher. I prayed that I would, but no such luck.

The worst of all our tortures was the tear-gas drill. Oh God, was that horrible as that gas seeped into our noses and eyes, burning like fire. I thought I was going to die. That's something you never forget.

Every day, our DI, Sergeant Hershey, screamed at us about being the stupidest bunch of misfits. "You people are the worst, the worst flight to ever go through Lackland!" It was true that we weren't very good at much of anything. We started out with about sixty girls in our flight, and we ended up with a little over thirty. Unlike the men, females washed out and got discharged if they couldn't handle it. They were the ones who cried all the time. I grabbed one of them one night (I couldn't sleep for her caterwauling) and hissed in her ear, "Dry it up, or I'll fix you so you can't cry! I mean, God, bawling isn't going to help." She was gone the next day.

My own roommate was a nut. She laughed all the time—yep, not making it up. She laughed and laughed. The DIs didn't like it, and boy, did they have fun with her before she washed out and I had a private room.

Back to Sergeant Hershey. I hated him so much that I came to the point that I told myself I would die before

I would let him get to me. So I became the super-troop, memorizing all the stuff we had to recite, all the marches we had to do. And, lo and behold, I found myself the barracks chief and the flight leader. There I was, just five four and leading a flight with women six feet tall.

Turned out that I loved marching; the precision of it was what I liked. I became a star on the parade grounds, and I ruled the barracks with an iron fist. Actually I just choked a couple of girls halfway unconscious and the others got the message. So, from the worst flight at Lackland AFB, we became—in less than eight weeks—the best flight at Lackland. I will always remember standing at attention on the parade ground before the base commander to receive our commendation. From the scraggly group we were to the team we had become was simply mind-boggling. We had lost 50 percent of our flight, but the 50 percent that remained were solid, and I was their leader. When I presented myself to the commander to be recognized, I was so proud I had to struggle not to smile. It was the greatest sense of pride I'd ever known.

Have you seen the movie *An Officer and A Gentleman* with Richard Gere? Well, when he went up to his DI after graduation, you could see the changed man that he was. It was the same for me. That DI I hated—Staff Sergeant Joe Hershey—actually he saved my life. Somehow, in those few weeks, he caused me to see what I could be and could do instead of who I had been. He showed me the power of small successes: the pair of combat boots that were shined to perfection, the starched uniform that was ironed flawlessly. I didn't know it then, but he was pivotal in my life. Without his driving influence, I would have ended up in prison.

Remember how I thought the Air Force would be my ticket to translating Russian? It was the height of the Cold War, and I was fluent in Russian, as tested by the air force itself. So I sat at Lackland anxiously awaiting my orders to Monterey, California (the location of the language school for the military). When my orders arrived, they told me the Air Force needed a clerk typist in Detroit. I said, "I don't type—never took it in high school. And besides, I grew up in Cleveland, so why would I want to go to Detroit?"

The sergeant looked at me with a funny grin and said, "You'll learn, airman. You'll learn."

So off to Detroit I went. Now, Detroit in those days was at war. Growing up in Cleveland, I never wanted to go Detroit; *nobody* wanted to go there. The whole city was off limits to air force personnel, and even the cops rode two to a car with the doors locked. So this is where my education really began.

I lost and regained the same stripe several times in my short tenure at Detroit. It was a Strategic Air Command (SAC) base, and it was the Cold War—Bay of Pigs. And I have to tell you, these people had *no* sense of humor. So when a prankster like me played a few tricks, the reaction was not what I expected. A favorite trick of mine went like this: I was very good with languages, and I could mimic voices very well. So I sometimes used these skills to pretend I was the base adjutant and ordered the commander's car to be brought around. Here came the commander's car, along with a whole retinue of things and people that accompanied the commander, horns blowing, flags waving, etc.—a big falderal, to say the least. Someone would finally ask where the commander was. Of course, there was no commander, and then all the caterwauling began. I would watch all this, secretly laughing my head off but careful not to give myself away. No one but me thought it was funny, but I was never caught.

Another stunt I pulled that *did* result in losing my one stripe was when a full-base alert was called in the middle of the night. I was sound asleep and had those old-fashioned rollers in my hair. (My hair has caused me *many* episodes of grief.) We had to be in full uniform and information within fifteen minutes. I knew I didn't have time to do all that and take the rollers out of my hair. So I showed up at a full-base alert with rollers in my hair and my Air Force cap sitting right on top of them. Hey, I was on time and in uniform, so what's the problem? Due to the lack of humor, I got gigged for being out of uniform. But, out of the corner of my eye, I did see my captain smile when he thought no one was looking.

As far as my religious state of mind through all this goes, I was angry with God. I don't think I ever didn't believe in God; I was just mad at him. I hadn't set foot in a church for a couple years—ever since that Lutheran dean had offered me a job as a prostitute. I just couldn't get my mind around God allowing horrible things to happen to people, especially kids—things often perpetrated by the very people who were supposed to take care of them.

One Sunday I went off base for a while (wasn't supposed to, but I did anyway), and I somehow found myself in front of a large Lutheran church. I walked into that church, saw that a service was in progress, and—I can't believe I did this—walked right up to the altar and knelt at the rope. Suddenly I was sobbing and sobbing uncontrollably. It was like all the misery of my childhood just poured out. I had no idea why I was there, sobbing loudly in front of hundreds of people, who were as quiet as church mice. I wondered years later what those people thought that Sunday when I walked into their routine, predictable Sunday service.

The point of this story is what happened next. As I knelt there with my head in my hands, crying, the Lutheran minister came over to me, put his hand on my head, and said, "My child, you are not alone." That comment has stayed in my mind ever since and sustained me through many trials yet to come. I've wondered so many times what that minister thought when I appeared in his church and if he had any idea what he did for me that morning.

When I was able, I got up and walked out, just like I'd walked in. I didn't go into a church again until years later.

I had my first date in Detroit. But first let me describe what happened to me right out of the gate. My first NCOIC (noncommissioned officer in charge) was a black man. Our first conversation began with him saying, "Airman, are you prejudiced?"

"No, sergeant, I am not prejudiced."

He quickly responded, "Well, then you'll go out with me!"

I looked at him and said, "But you're married, and I don't go out with married men." I thought I nailed that one, but he had other ideas and began chasing me around the desk in his office. I told him to get away from me or I'd start screaming, and he backed off. But then, that week, I got transferred out of his squadron. This was not good, because it implied that I did something wrong. Still, I was glad to get away from him.

I found out the next day that my new OIC (officer in charge) was a female captain. I was excited about this and was anxious to meet her. She seemed okay and was rather homely, with short, straight black hair and dark eyes. She wasn't a lot bigger than me. Things went along pretty good for a couple of weeks, and then she told me she wanted me to help her with some extra work, so she wanted me to meet her in the parking lot that night. Honest to God, I never thought anything about it, but remember that I never dated at all.

I met her that night, and she said she was going to take us to another location where we could get this work done more conveniently. So I got in her car. Well, I didn't know anything about being gay, but I sure found out in a hurry. She reached for my blouse saying "let's see those tits". I was out of that car and running so fast that I don't remember if I closed the door or not. I don't even remember opening it! This was a new paradigm for me. So, after a lot of paperwork, I got transferred again. Things weren't going well for me in Detroit, but at least the abuse was over.

But was it? As a result of my childhood, I was severely claustrophobic—left over from the nights in the cellar. And I didn't like being touched by anyone anywhere. So I wasn't normal at all. The good news was that my job had settled down, and I became a pretty good clerk typist in an office with five men. My sergeant was a great guy. He did everything he could to help me, but I was too busy ruining my life to listen to him. Sergeant J. B. Arund was Danish with blond hair and blue eyes. He was short and stocky but a real sweetheart behind his tough-guy façade. I was invited to dinner at his home with his family on several occasions. These were great memories for me sprinkled among the nightmares.

He worked with me on my application to Officer School, and I made it. But then I got myself pregnant (more about that later). Did I mention that I really did learn to type? Pretty well, too. We had those horrible purple mimeograph papers then that got all over your hands and clothes. They put a trash can as big as my body at my desk, gave me reams of paper and the Air Force manual on typing, and said, "Go to it, airman." Many trash cans later, I actually could do my job pretty well, which was to type correspondence for the people in my office as well as type Top Secret documents.

I still remember the excitement on that base due to the escalation of the Cold War. Our bombers were fully loaded and in the air around the clock. When one of those B-52s landed, the ground shook. It was an awesome thing to see and hear. And I have to admit I was proud to be a part of it, even if it was a small part.

I also got assigned my weekly KP (kitchen) duties, like everyone else, although not all the duties were in the kitchen. I'll never forget what happened to me during that duty assignment—and probably all the others who saw it never will either. My sergeant told me to patrol the parking lot outside our building and to pick up all the litter and put it in a big bag. That's exactly what I did.

Keep in mind this was the early sixties, and we didn't wear gloves or use one of those sticks—just our hands.

The problem was that I didn't know what I was picking up. But I sure found out when Sarge came running out of the office, yelling, "Airman, airman, what are you doing?"

I thought that was an absurd question, but I said, "Sarge, I'm doing what you told me to do: cleaning up the parking lot. What's wrong?"

I saw a look come over his face as he said, "You don't know what those things are, do you?"

"What, these little plastic tube-looking things?" "Airman," he said. Then he leaned toward me and whispered, "Those things are rubbers—you know— what men wear when they have sex." Not only had I never seen one, I had never even heard of one. I know my face turned beet red, and I was halfway sick to my stomach on top of being royally embarrassed. I dropped everything and ran to the john. I think I came close to scrubbing off the top layer of my skin before I could let it go. Sarge never said another word to me about the incident, which spoke volumes of his kindness.

Then I really got myself in a sticky wicket with an incident that started out as a fun adventure. My friends and I decided that a picnic would be just what we needed, so we left base and headed to a place at one of the local rivers. There were six of us—three girls and three guys, as I remember. We were dressed in civilian clothes and stopped at a convenience store to pick up what we needed.

One of the guys was Jack, the kid that had asked me for a date that I mentioned before. He wasn't particularly good-looking, but he was tall. He was balding, too—no

Richard Gere. And he was always blabbing about Kansas, where he came from. But he was the first guy who had ever expressed an interest in me, so we had been out a couple of times.

Back to the picnic. Everything was going per usual—hot dogs, beer—and when we had full bellies, it was time for games. That's when I came up with a scheme to push Jack into the river. I didn't like him much anyway—he was a know-it-all. So I snuck up behind him to give him a shove into the river. Well, my plan went astray when he saw me coming out of the corner of his eye and sidestepped so that I was the one who ended up falling in the river.

Everyone laughed themselves sick, because I looked like a drowned rat. The girls held up a blanket so I could get out of my wet clothes. But I had only one dry piece of clothing left, and that was my air force raincoat. So that's what I put on. We headed back to the base, still in a carefree and happy state of mind, until I almost puked when I saw the sign at the gate announcing that the base was on full alert. I knew immediately that we would have to stand inspection. "Yikes, I'm out of uniform!" I yelled. "If they ask me to open my raincoat, what am I going to do?" Everyone got very quiet, because we all knew this was a bad portent.

So, to make a long story short, we had to stand at attention while the guards searched our vehicle and then lined us up for inspection. That was standard protocol due to our Cold War status. When they got to me, the guard told me to open my raincoat. I had to choose between refusing to follow an order or being out of uniform (actually being naked under the raincoat). For a few tortuous seconds, I went back and forth on those two options. I chose to open my raincoat as ordered because, in my mind, the guards were guys and would handle my nakedness better than they would handle my refusal to follow an order.

I unbuttoned my raincoat, opened it, and stood at attention. I couldn't see all their reactions, but the two in front of me were visibly stunned, and their eyes were glued on my body. After a few seconds, the senior-ranking guard told me to button my raincoat then asked me what had happened. So I told him. He told all of us to get out of there. I ran as fast as I could, hoping never to see those guards again or even my friends. My face was red as a beet and as hot as fire. I just wanted to hide somewhere. Amazingly, I never heard a thing about this incident again—except from Jack and the others, who delighted in dragging me through it over and over.

Speaking of Jack, we were dating regularly. He was getting serious, and he made his move. I'll never know why I let him, because I felt no emotion for him at all. But I let him—there in his car right on base. It was basically a wham- bam kind of deal with no concern for me at all.

Of course, I got pregnant, so there went my plans to attend Officer Candidate School. I not only ruined my future, I also sorely disappointed Sergeant Arund. I ended up marrying Jack for no real reason other than being pregnant and what I many years later identified was the classic girl marrying an abuser just like her father. I certainly couldn't go home.

So I went from the frying pan to the fire. In those days, a female in the Air Force had to separate from the service when she married or got pregnant. Men didn't have to do that. Discrimination again! Sergeant Arund looked so sad when I said goodbye. I've thought of him many times over the years. He really did have my best interests at heart. So I married Jack Hartle in a Justice of the Peace wedding—nothing special and no honeymoon or anything else.

Then Jack told me he was getting out of the Air Force and we were going back to his beloved Kansas. He wanted to take his bride home. Together we began the long drive from Detroit to Dry Gulch, Kansas. Yes, Dry Gulch. I should have known where this was going.

CHAPTER 4

THE KANSAS ADVENTURE BEGINS

After what seemed like endless days of driving and nights in dirty, cheap motels, we arrived in Dry Gulch. When I look back on this chapter of my life, I still shudder. A popular TV show in those days was a Western called *Gunsmoke*, starring Matt Arness as Marshal Dillon. In the TV series, the town had wooden sidewalk; lots of dust, grime, and dirt; unpaved streets; and people who looked like their last bath was months ago. Well, that's what I saw as we drove down the dusty, unpaved main road of Dry Gulch. There were no stop lights—or stop signs, for that matter. The sidewalks were indeed wooden, and there was one general store that seemed to be open. Only around a hundred people lived in that desolate place, and now there would be 102.

Coming from big cities in the Northeast, I had cultural shock. But that was only the beginning. We drove to the house where my in-laws lived. It was—for lack of an adequate description—a shanty. Paint was peeling off the walls—where there was paint. The yard was unmowed, and the doors to the house were wide open. It was also sweltering at 112 degrees. It was August, I was pregnant, and I had never experienced temperatures over 90 degrees.

Not much fun so far, but the worst was yet to come. That happened when we started into the house and I met my father-in-law, John. He was short, and to say he was fat would be an understatement. He was almost as wide as he was tall, bald with glasses, and when he smiled, it was clear most of his teeth were gone. Worst of all, I had no idea what the hell was running down his chin, having never seen tobacco chewed in my life.

Then he started toward me, and—oh my God—he wanted to hug me. *Don't touch me! Don't come near me. I need to get out of here!* screamed in my mind. But my feet were nailed to the ground. He grabbed me and hugged me tightly. "Welcome, Susan. Welcome to our home," he said, smiling at me. I was stiff with horror.

We walked inside, and I couldn't believe my eyes. There was clutter everywhere; I couldn't tell where to safely put my feet as I tried to walk. There were sheets over the windows, and wallpaper was peeling off the walls. It was also unbelievably hot. When I found out there were no bathing facilities in the house, I thought, *No shower? Where in the hell am I anyway?* I knew I had been bad growing up—never told about my father, almost killed my best friend—but did I deserve this?

Then I saw the kitchen and almost threw up. Food was in dishes under a tablecloth on the kitchen table. Jack's mother, Mary, removed the tablecloth so we could eat, and roaches ran everywhere. Now, I didn't know these bugs were roaches until later, because I had never seen a roach before. But I knew this wasn't good, healthy, or clean, and my mind reeled with these horrible sights.

While my mind was struggling with all this, Mary made the mistake of grabbing my arm. "Susan, welcome to our home," she said, and she started to hug me.

I hissed, "Don't touch me"! That was my first interaction with my mother-in-law. She wasn't a bad person, and things improved with time, but we were never close. I think we all know why.

Even though I briefly mentioned my mother's dirt phobia earlier, I didn't explain to you what my life was like with her, the bionic cleaning woman. My mother's nickname was Irma Immaculate, and it was no joke. You could literally eat off her floors, because we scrubbed them all once a week. The kitchen and bathroom floors were scrubbed daily. Did I say scrubbed? It was more like scoured.

Mother's regimen set me up for basic training in the military better than anyone could imagine. It also set me up to be a flaming obsessive-compulsive. Dad and I weren't allowed in the living room unless we'd just had our baths or there was company. And this next part you won't believe: My mother considered a woman's menses to be vile, so when that time of month came, I had to go to the unheated outside garage to change my pads—in Cleveland! Thank God my period didn't start until I was seventeen.

I think you can see how traumatic this Kansas nightmare was to me. And then I found out I had to live there. I'm not sure how I didn't lose my mind—really. I couldn't sleep for worrying about those bugs, and I didn't eat anything that wasn't in a can or a bottle—and unopened. Did I tell you about their refrigerator? It didn't have a seal around the door, and the roaches were in there, too. It was worse than my worst nightmare—bugs crawling on me! Even the cellar didn't have bugs!

This went on for several months. I was sick from the heat a lot, especially as my pregnancy developed. The doc had me on salt pills, but I was miserable. It was 110 degrees or over every frigging day, and all they had were a couple of fans.

Then there were the tornadoes. I remember the first one vividly. It was pouring rain, and the lightning was huge— like it is in the Midwest, where the sky goes on forever. I was sitting on the bed in the room my husband and I lived in when his father, John, ran into the room and told me we had to go to the storm cellar because a tornado was on the way. The whole family started getting ready to run outside and down into the storm cellar. (There were still two kids living at home with John and Mary.) I sat on the edge of that broken-down bed and decided I wasn't going.

As they started by me, they yelled, "C'mon, we have to go."

I shook my head, crossed my arms, and said, "No, I'm not going. I'd rather blow away than go down there."

You know why, don't you? Remember where I spent my young childhood—in a dark cellar? I was claustrophobic as a result of that terror. Besides, it was Kansas, and there were rattlesnakes down in that cellar. John told me that all we had to do was make a lot of noise, and the snakes would go away. I had absolutely no faith in that—true or not true.

So they went down into the cellar, and I sat on the edge of the bed. I have to admit, it was pretty scary. The wind, the hail, the noise was deafening, but I stayed on that bed, and it stayed on the floor. Then it was over, and the rains stopped and the sky cleared. The family came back from the cellar, shaking their heads at me as they walked by my bed. Keep in mind that this was where my husband and I slept, but the whole family walked right through it whenever they went out and in through the back door. There was no privacy at all.

The family went to the grandfather's house for their baths. Didn't that kind of stuff end in the 1800s? I struggled with thoughts like this and had no one to talk to about them. Jack, who should have been with me to help me adapt to this new hell, was nowhere to be found, having taken up with his old friends to play pool and go coon hunting. I had no idea what that was, and when I found out, I couldn't understand why anyone would want to spend time chasing raccoons. They made hats out of them and even ate them. I'd starve to death first!

I found out that Mary worked in the fields in her bare feet. She was a hard worker and preferred fieldwork to housework. That was no surprise. At the end of the day, she took a wet cloth and wiped her feet off. That pretty much summed up her hygiene. I thought about my mother so many times and wondered what was right: her way, this way, what way? I was very confused with all of it.

I felt like I was going crazy. That horrible place, those dirty people, the heavy homesickness, and the great sadness I felt were weighing down on me. I started to turn inward, refusing to talk to anyone. I sat in one rocking chair all day long and just rocked. At one point, I started banging my head on the wall. I didn't know it then, but I was slipping into another world.

My father-in-law was the only one who tried to reach me. He was very kind, even if he looked horrible. Though I didn't respond to him, he got through to me. One day I saw an ad in a newspaper lying on the table that said there was a psychiatrist making rounds to various small towns and that this service was free to those without the means to pay. Somehow I knew I needed to go there, so I asked my father- in-law to take me. So we went, my father-in-law and me.

I walked into the office and told the person at the desk that I needed to speak to the psychiatrist and that I had no money. She told me to sit down and fill out some papers. I did and then I waited—never thinking for one moment what I was going to say or even why I was there. When it was my turn, I went into the psychiatrist's office and saw a kind- looking, middle-aged woman sitting there. She had warm brown eyes and a kind smile. She asked me to sit down. Then she said, "Tell me why you're here and what is wrong." I told her I didn't know, but then it was like a huge gate opened up. I poured out my whole story from the time I arrived in Cleveland, Ohio, as a five-year old. She never interrupted me as I went on and on. For how long? I have no idea. When I finished my whole life history, I looked at her and asked her one question: "Am I crazy?"

In retrospect, that doctor could have said a million different things, but what she said was the beginning of my healing process. She looked at me so warmly and smiled as she said, "My dear child, you are not crazy at all. You have simply lived through more hell in your short eighteen years than most people see in a lifetime." Those words played over and over in my mind for many years, and every time I replayed them, I was reminded that I was okay. It was a light in my life to show me the way.

As my pregnancy advanced, I saw less and less of the man I'd married. All these years later, I can't remember a single conversation with him—only fights because I wouldn't do whatever he wanted me to do. Somehow, though, a miracle occurred. We managed to get a small upstairs apartment in Jones, a town nearby. This town was bigger, and it even had stores! The apartment actually had running water, a tub, a kitchen, and a separate bedroom. Jack was gone most of the time, and I was so happy to have a place where I could be alone. When Jack was there, he slept. He spent most nights playing pool. When he was around, especially when he'd been drinking, he was abusive to me.

His pool-hall money was how we paid for the apartment, so that was fine by me. I had no phone, no TV, no radio, and no car. I spent my time walking all over Jones, looking in windows and dreaming of what it would be like to have pretty things. I begged every store owner for a job, but there were none to be had in that small town. When I wasn't walking, I was cleaning. I scrubbed that apartment from top to bottom almost every other day. I had learned much from my mother.

I had no maternity clothes, so I was pinning my skirts together and wore my shirts pulled out over those skirts, which I'd had for years. I had no baby clothes or anything.

Most of all, I had no food. I'm serious. No food. I was hungry. Maybe you don't know what it's like to be really hungry—not just for a day but every day, day after day. You get to where you dream about food, and you can smell it in your dreams.

On good days, there was some money to buy a few things to eat—I'm talking bread or crackers. Best of all, I remember my father-in-law showing up once in a while with grocery sacks of regular food. I loved those visits. As a result of having very little food, I gained only eight and a half pounds with my pregnancy, and my baby weighed eight pounds and one ounce. So that tells that story!

I walked and I walked, knowing people wondered who I was and what was wrong with me. I talked to no one except Grandma Martin, who lived in the apartment right across from me. She was kind to me, so I did speak to her on occasion. But I never told her I was hungry or that my husband beat me. Yes, I married the perfect man to continue my father's abuse! I never thought one thought about that when I agreed to marry this man. I have no clear idea why I even married him, because I never loved him or even liked him. I guess I have to leave that to the psychiatrists.

I was so confused, so sad and so lonely. No one to talk to – didn't even know how to start if I did have someone. When I thought about my life, it just seemed more and more to my tortured mind that I didn't belong in this world. Without ever telling anyone what I was thinking and feeling, I slipped into another world where death was attractive and I thought about ways to die and how I would be in a better world along with my unborn baby.

Unless you've lived with abject hopelessness, you'll never understand what it is like to entertain suicidal thoughts.

So, it was, I suppose, inevitable that one day I simply turned on the gas burners on the kitchen stove and laid down on the couch in the small living room next to the kitchen. I said the Lord's Prayer for me and for my baby and fell asleep. I never once dreamed that Jack would come home early that day but he did. He found me unconscious and called the ambulance. God had intervened, although I had no idea why. Staff at the hospital worked with me so I wouldn't do that again but Jack never spoke of it. Our lives together, if you could say that we had lives together, continued on as they had.

One of the things that I enjoyed while I lived in Jones was the small Lutheran church there. I felt awful because I didn't have money to put in the collection hat. But I went there because that was the one place I felt good. The minister showed much insight into how to work with people like me. Rather than telling me I didn't have to be concerned about being broke, he told me he needed a volunteer to wash dishes on certain days. I jumped on that, because I didn't feel like a moocher. So we had a deal that worked for the short time we lived in that community.

One day I had the best surprise next to food: I got a letter from Johnny. I tore it open, as I missed our dancing and his soft voice. "Chicky, I hope you are doing all right. I'm in the army—got drafted—and it looks like Vietnam for me. Miss you and the cool dancing we did together. Every time I hear 'One, two, three o'clock, four o'clock, rock,' I remember us dancing at American Bandstand! You are the best dancer ever—Johnny." I treasured that letter for many years and often thought about Johnny. I prayed that he wouldn't get killed in Nam.

In my real world, my biggest worry was that I still had nothing for my baby to wear and no food either. I was due in two to three weeks. My mother, back home in Cleveland, was working in a sewing factory at the time, making baby clothes, and I was thrilled to get some adorable outfits from her one day. My baby's first clothes! I didn't know what to do about everything else I needed and was ashamed to tell anyone.

One morning, I opened my apartment door to go for my walk, and there sat a bassinette completely packed with baby clothes, diapers, and everything I would possibly need. I sat there in the hallway and cried and cried. Grandma Martin must have heard me, because she opened her door and consoled me. I wondered many times if she was behind the whole thing or if it was the women from the church. Regardless of who did it, I was very grateful for this miracle for my unborn baby, who would now have outfits and diapers like other babies and a bassinet to sleep in instead of the dresser drawer I was going to use.

I was alone, as usual, in the apartment when a gripping pain hit my whole right side and circled around to my back. I stopped what I was doing, grabbed my side, and the pain went away—only to return in a few minutes. It hurt more and more. I didn't even think of labor; it just hurt. I started to cry, because I didn't know what to do or what it was.

Finally, I went over to Grandma Martin's apartment and told her what was happening. I will always remember what she said as she smiled at me and patted me on my arm, "Well, honey, it's your time. Your labor has started!" I was shocked and scared. I didn't know what to do, but Grandma Martin did. She asked where my husband was, and I said, "I didn't know—probably at the pool hall."

"Tsk, tsk," she said as she shook her head and picked up her phone to call a cab for me. Soon I was on the way to the hospital.

In retrospect, my labor experience was normal, except that I was so alone and so scared. I had no idea, really, what was happening to my body and had no one to talk to or reassure me. One or two of the OB staff talked to me a little, but mostly I felt like I was in a strange world all by myself. They gave me enemas—can you imagine enemas when you're in labor?! That's cruel! But I suffered through them.

Then my father-in-law showed up. I've never known how he knew to come to the hospital, but it was probably Grandma Martin again. John stayed with me throughout the rest of my labor, and I squeezed his hand so hard I thought he would tell me to stop, but he never did. After about twelve hours, I was ready for the delivery room— thank God. They told me later that my amniotic sac was so tough they had to cut it open. They said it was because I walked so much; they didn't know I'd been an athlete.

They came to me with a little baby all wrapped up and put it in my arms—and it was a little girl. Wow! I hadn't expected a girl. (In those days, there was no way to know until the baby was born.) My little girl had black hair all over her head, her shoulders, and her forehead. I had chosen the name Valerie, but when I looked at her, I decided her name should be Sally.

A few hours later, Jack showed up and went to see our baby. I was exhausted and angry and didn't want to see him. I mean, where was he when I needed him?

I thought I was going back to the apartment but was devastated when I found out Jack hadn't paid the rent, so I couldn't go back there. My baby and I had to go back to Dry Gulch and my in-laws' horrible home. If I'd had anyone to call or any money, I would have been gone. I had no one to talk to and nowhere else to go, so it was back at that awful place with my beautiful baby girl.

Remember the roaches that were all over this house? I mean, the place should have been burned down. Roaches everywhere—and my little baby girl, Sally, exposed to that. She was such a sweet baby who never cried unless she was hungry. The first night there, I was sound asleep and woke up to her screaming, so I turned on the light in our bedroom (a.k.a. Grand Central Station) and saw a living nightmare: roaches were crawling on my baby's face—all over her face!

Something snapped in my brain, and I went wacko. I grabbed my baby, got the roaches off her, and ran through the house, turning all the lights on and yelling, "Get up, you sonsabitches. You're going to kill these roaches." So, somewhere around two in the morning, I had everyone in that household out of bed, swatting at roaches. Every single one of them was killing roaches except my husband, who was gone with his buddies, as usual. I was temporarily wacko, and I think I scared the shit out of everyone in that sad excuse for a house.

Then, amazingly, my husband got a real job—driving a truck cross-country. For reasons unknown to me, we had to move to a really small town in northern New Mexico called Carver—even smaller than Dry Gulch. We found a one-room upstairs apartment. It was tiny, but there were no roaches, and it had running water. I had gone up in the world!

Jack was gone more than he was there (joy!), and I spent my time taking care of my daughter (now about eight months old), taking care of myself (now about five months pregnant), and again we had little to eat. The worst part was that it wasn't just me who was hungry—it was little Sally, too. Again I walked the town every day, just looking at stuff. I was pretty sure I was the only "Norte Americana gringa" in the whole town. When I walked through the one general store, there were all these Mexicans guys sitting on the floor, and their eyes followed me. They would say sexist things in Spanish, not knowing I understood them.

When Jack was home, things were always tense. I guess he sensed I didn't really love him or even like him. Fights were par for the course, usually ending up with him punching me, or whatever. I didn't help matters because I behaved like a banty rooster, which incited him even more. One night we got into a fight over money. "I need some money when you're gone, Jack," I implored. "Things happen, and you're not here to help."

"You have all you need. What do you think I'm going to do when I'm on the road? I need the money to buy food. I'm working! You always want something. Get a job and quit mooching."

That made me see red, and I went for him. "I hate you," I screeched as I punched him in the gut. I could see I surprised him with the force I had and that I would even dare to hit him as big as he was—six two to my five four.

He grabbed me, overpowering me easily, like always, and slammed me against the wall. I bounced off it, and he grabbed me again and shoved me. That caused me to lose my balance, and I fell down a flight of stairs. I was very lucky not to lose my baby, but I had a very sore back for days. Of course, I didn't have the luxury of medical care, not for that or for prenatal care or anything else. I later learned that the fall caused a small fracture in my thoracic spine, which caused me much discomfort as I got older.

On my daily walks through Carver, I frequently saw a woman who came into town, always dressed in navy blue and always carrying a black leather bag that looked like something a doctor would carry. I didn't meet her but learned later that she was a public health nurse. I didn't know it at the time, but she was watching me more than I was watching her. I saw her go into that general store every day she came to town. I couldn't figure out what she was up to or who she was, but something about her demeanor made me feel like she was someone official.

Anyway, that winter was harsh—colder than I ever spent anywhere, even Ohio. It was *brutally* cold. Sally and I still walked when we could. After all, I had no phone, no TV, no car, and no radio. It was just the two of us— well, three. Then my little girl and I got sick. We had such poor nutrition and it was so cold in that apartment, it was no wonder. The woman who owned the building lived downstairs and had the heat controls in her apartment. I figured that she was an alcoholic who drank herself into a stupor every night, but not before she turned the heat off for the whole building. Meanwhile, little Sally and I were freezing, even though I had a snowsuit on her and my own coat on me inside the apartment.

I didn't know what it was until later, but my little girl and I got the Asian flu that was going around that year. The vomiting and diarrhea were awful for both of us. The last thing I remember was lying in the bed in the apartment, my little girl asleep in her snowsuit and me with my coat on. I don't know what happened next except for what I was told. As it turns out, that woman that seemed official to me was. She was a public health nurse. She knew something was wrong when she didn't see Sally and me out walking. She asked the old men in the general store, and they said they hadn't seen me for days. She then found out where our apartment was and got the sheriff to go with her.

I was told that they knocked down the door to get to me, because the landlady was still in a drunken stupor. My little girl and I were both unconscious and were rushed by ambulance to the hospital in Tucumcari, New Mexico. When I woke up, in that hospital bed, the first thing I saw was an old man with white hair sitting beside my bed with a stethoscope around his neck. He had kind eyes, and I asked him if my baby was okay. He smiled and said that all three of us were going to be fine.

I learned later from the nurses that, in their opinion, I would have died that night if it weren't for the doctor, who stayed at my side all night long. They said he knew my little girl would be okay but was afraid I wouldn't make it, along with my unborn child.

You know, one of my regrets is that I never got that doctor's name and never thanked him for the lives of my children and me. How I wish I had. Same for the public health nurse—making her rounds and doing what public health nurses do: observing and reporting, observing and taking action. I never got her name, though she saved all our lives.

When my husband finally showed up, he decided he was going back to Kansas, so there's where we went. I hated him and my life so much, it didn't even matter anymore. If I had anywhere to go, I'd have been there.

Shortly after our return to Kansas, my labor began. I didn't want to have any more babies because (a) I couldn't feed them, and (b) labor hurt like hell. Well, this time, I was in for an even better treat. I had been in labor for two days and was exhausted and scared when the nurse did another pelvic exam. I heard her whisper to the aide with her, "We have to get her doctor. The baby is lying in a transverse position, and all I can feel are the fingers of one hand."

That's not going to work, my brain said.

When he got there, my doctor decided not to give me a C-section. Instead he rotated the baby manually—without anesthesia. He had one hand/arm in my vagina through my cervix and the other on my abdomen so he could rotate the baby into a position where the baby could be born. This was one of the few times I screamed. And scream I did. The anesthetist who was going to put me to sleep was a nun, and she kept telling me to be quiet and that it was going to be all right. "How do you know?" I yelled at her.

It's amazing what human beings can tolerate and survive. Survive I did. But it didn't get better. Jack showed up and pulled up a chair by my bed, all smiles. He reached over to pat my arm, and I raised up and hissed, "Don't touch me, you bastard. Get the hell out of here." And I turned my back to him.

The next morning, I was scheduled to go home when a funny thing happened. I heard my roommate tell her doctor she wanted birth control pills. My ears perked right up! I didn't know there was such a thing, but I knew that was what I needed. When my barbarian doctor showed up, I told him the same thing. At least it would give me the opportunity to control what would happen to me in regard to having more children. The doc said he would consider that at my six-month checkup. Wrong answer! I harshly replied, "Just last night you told me I was in bad shape and had to stay in the hospital for a week—until I reminded you that I have no insurance. Then you said I could leave today. Now I'm telling you I'm not leaving here without those pills, because by six months from now, I'll be pregnant again!" I got my birth control pills. Over the years I would hear women talk about how they forgot to take their birth control pill. I never came close to missing one and couldn't fathom how anyone could.

I'll remember forever the moment the nurse brought my son to me. As I laid my eyes on him the first time, I was stunned and actually felt a shock go through my body as I said words out loud that I didn't even know I knew. As I looked down at him tucked in my arm, I whispered,

"He's star-crossed." I learned what that expression meant later. Over his youth and early adulthood, it became obvious, but how I knew it at that moment I've never understood. I guess I should have; in his very young life, he had already almost died twice.

So, there I was, with two hungry babies so close in age that people often thought they were twins and a husband who didn't provide anything on a regular basis to support us. Worst of all was the hunger—not just me but my two children, too. Just to make sure you get it: I'm not talking about a few hours of being hungry or being hungry off and on. I'm talking about getting up hungry and going to bed hungry day after day.

I dreamed about my favorite foods many nights. But the worst was hearing my babies cry, especially my newborn son, who had no milk. They gave me a shot in the hospital to dry up my milk without asking me, so I couldn't nurse him. The few dollars my husband shared whenever he wanted to, plus the wonderful times when my father-in-law, John, showed up with groceries, kept us from dying from starvation. But it did not stop the ever-present, gnawing hunger that was a part of our lives way too long. These were the days before all the massive Medicaid programs were available. I went to various agencies looking for help for my babies but didn't qualify for any of them for reasons that made no sense to me and just caused me to become even angrier. Finally, at one agency, after they told me I didn't qualify, I just sat down on the floor with my two babies. "I'm not going anywhere until you give me some money for food for my babies", I spat. I didn't think of it at the time, but it was the first sit- down strike I ever heard of and I did it! Well, after a few minutes, a staff worker approached me and said that they were going to give me money for food. "What did you say", I stammered, not believing my ears. "Here it is, - $45 – but you can't buy cigarettes or candy with it", she admonished as she helped me off the floor.

I was ecstatic - $45 went a long way then. I never smoked and while I loved candy, this money was for the kids more than anything else.

We also moved again but this time to a bigger town called Centerville. We rented an actual house with separate rooms – that was all great! But then I learned that there was no running water or toilets in the house! And … when the wind blew (frequently in Kansas), my baby son's bassinett blew across the room!

Ironically, a local doctor owned it, and we actually paid rent. Think about preparing infant formula and washing diapers (no disposables for me) with no indoor water.

Jack was home almost all the time, having sustained some kind of injury that hurt his back. So now he was in pain, which did nothing good for his mood. Let me point out that he still went hunting and fishing, and he still played his precious pool. Jack was a miserable man, and he beat me on a regular basis, once breaking my glasses on my face so that I had to go to the local ER and have glass picked out of my skin and my eyelids.

I hated him so much but didn't know what to do. I had nowhere to go, and I had my two little babies. One day, I did something that made him angry with me. (I probably lipped off to him.) He got so mad, he screamed he was going to kill me. I ran and hid in the closet (not very bright, I know, but fear doesn't produce clear thinking). He, of course, found me, yanked the door open, and punched me right in the face with his fist. I saw stars but didn't pass out. Of course my nose was broken—again.

Later that night, when he in a drunken stupor, I decided to kill him. God forbid, but I did want to kill him. I went into the kitchen, got a butcher knife, and headed back to the bedroom, where he was sprawled across the bed. The kids were asleep in the other room. I got in a good position to be able to stab him right in the chest and had the knife in both hands as high as I could reach. I hesitated a second and then started to bring the knife down—and he woke up. I saw his eyes react to what he was seeing, and in a second, he grabbed my hands, wrestled the knife away from me, and beat the crap out of me.

I went to bed and sobbed for hours. I had no remorse for what I had tried to do. All I could think of was that there was no way out for me. Sometimes I thought this horrible life happened to me to punish me for what happened with my father. I was being punished for not telling anyone, or I was a bad person and this was my penance. Wow, I had a heavy dose of Irish Catholicism, right?

Despite all this, my life had been full of miracles, and that's what I chose to focus on as much as I could. Look at the good, not the bad! So another miracle came my way in the person of a woman I met through my husband's coworker, Marylee. Marylee knew my situation and asked me if I wanted a job at one of the local hospitals. I told her

I absolutely would. I'd never wanted to work in a hospital, but we were hungry.

So off I went to get this job, and get it I did. It wasn't easy, because the director of nursing wanted someone experienced. I begged her, really. I pleaded with her to give me a chance, telling her my children were hungry. I had my two babies with me and I'm sure we looked pathetic. I was so relieved when she nodded okay. Eureka, I had a job! It was the three-to-eleven shift, but that was good because my friend worked that shift, too, and would give me a ride when she could.

I didn't know it at the time, but Marylee, her husband, Leland, and their three sons, Nate, Harry, and Joe, would be a part of our lives through the years. These people held up the light for me at the darkest moments to show me the way. Without Marylee and her family, I'm convinced I would never have survived—or my kids either.

My orientation for being a nurse's aide in an acute care hospital began unobtrusively but didn't stay that way for long. They handed me a mint-green pinafore and told me to watch for the lights to come on over each patient's door. When they did, I was to go and see what the patient needed. It sounded fairly simple, but true to my sordid life experiences so far, it didn't work out that way.

As I opened the door to answer the first call light that came on, I barely missed being hit in the head by a flying bedpan—yes, an airborne bedpan. In those days, the bedpans were stainless steel, and this one wasn't empty. As the contents of that bedpan hit the wall and the door and me, it was all I could do not to vomit right there. The smell was so awful (even after diapers for the last two years) that I was sickened. And I had to clean that all up and listen to the tirade of the very angry patient. He was just angry with his plight in life and taking it out on whoever got in his path.

I guess I don't have to say that if it weren't for the fact that my two babies were hungry, I would have been out of there at that very moment. God knows I wanted to go home, but I didn't. For the next six to eight months, I forced myself to go to work day after day. The only good thing was the money I got paid every Friday: $1.01 an hour. I was absolutely gleeful on my first payday. I smiled at Marylee and said, "I have my own money."

"Well, don't give him one red cent," she told me. "This is for you and the kids. You worked for it!" It was my first real paycheck since the military, and it was mine. My kids and I could eat on a regular basis. I felt tears on my face before I even knew I was crying—tears of joy and relief.

You wouldn't believe the fun we had on that three-to-eleven shift, but only when our work was done. We were a close-knit group that looked out for each other and worked together to get all our work done. One of the things we did for fun was to fill 50cc syringes with water and splat each other in the back every chance we got. One of the evening supervisors was a hawk for things like this, and she almost caught us more than once. But we were too good for her. Those water fights were the best. Years later, whenever we saw each other, we laughed about our adventures there.

Other adventures happened, too. We always met in one patient's room. She was unconscious and had been for twenty-two years. She had been in a car accident, and her husband, a local physician, paid to keep her in that hospital room. Even more amazing, she never had any skin breakdown. Her care was so good, her skin remained in excellent condition right up to her death over twenty-two years later.

We met in her room because she couldn't tell anyone. "Jamie, let's go get a burger after work," I said to our three-to-eleven orderly. I'm hungry!" So we now had something to look forward to. I liked Jamie. He was cute, but most of all, he was funny. "Kiddo, for having two kids, you look real nice—tight buns, too," he said as he felt me up right there in that patient's room. Then he surprised me when he reached up and took my glasses off. "Your eyes are stunning," he whispered. I loved it and felt really good.

I also met a couple at work that became family friends— Lee Ann and Caldwell Johnson. Caldwell was my patient, and I thought I killed him one evening. He had been in a car accident, and both his ankles and lower legs were broken in several places. He had bilateral casts. Caldwell was a large man, and I had to use a contraption called a Hoyer lift to move him from place to place in his room. It was the first time I'd used the thing. When I had him positioned right over his bed, I released the knob that controlled the movement of the lift so he would descend to his bed. Only problem is that I released the knob completely instead of gradually. Seeing Caldwell's legs in those casts hit that mattress and bounce up and down was very scary. I knew I either killed him or broke his legs again. He bounced up and down for what seemed like forever.

Funny thing is that no one made a sound. I was frozen in time, watching this horrible event and thinking I'd lost my job. Caldwell was as quiet as death. Finally, his legs stopping bouncing up and down, and he stayed in place on the bed. I stepped around the lift and asked him how his legs were. "Well, Susan, I think I'm okay, and I think my legs are okay, too—no thanks to you."

"I know," I breathed. "I thought I had killed you. I am so sorry, Caldwell, so sorry." I checked his legs. "I'll get the nurse right away."

They x-rayed his legs, and thank God, there were no new breaks and everything was still where it was supposed to be. What a relief I felt, and Caldwell, too! They had in-serviced me on this Hoyer lift so I can't claim I didn't know what to do. It was simply a matter of not remembering how to release the knob—one small thing that almost hurt a patient. I never forgot the lesson I learned: demonstrate your knowledge of how to use a piece of equipment with a mentor before using it with a patient.

Every evening I had to get Caldwell's food trays ready for him to eat. I can't tell you how hard it was for me to prepare that food and give it to him, because I was so very hungry. My meager salary, although much appreciated, didn't go far. Then he wouldn't eat all of it, and I had to throw it away. As hard as it was, I never let myself take any of that food. I felt that if I did that, I would lose all my dignity. But, unbeknownst to me, Caldwell's mother saw all of this, and I later learned that she told her son that I didn't have enough food to eat. What they did is simply beautiful: together they planned ways to get me to accept food she brought to the hospital "for my kids."

That worked, and it was wonderful to take home some homemade soup or homemade chicken and noodles like they make in the South. I will never forget the first time I tasted those noodles.

Well, suffice it to say that, after everything we went through, we became lifelong friends. Caldwell and his mother, Lee Ann, came to get the kids and me every weekend and took us for a car ride that always ended up with us eating something somewhere. My children loved those outings, as did I. Then we started going to their home, where we played games and—of course—ate!

I usually walked to work and walked home, but on occasion, my friends would offer me a ride as long as my husband wasn't around. Everyone was afraid of Jack—for good reason: he was a violent man. I wasn't afraid of him, but I should have been. Sometimes being courageous gets you in worse situations.

One night a couple of guys from work took me home, and they took me to the government housing where I now lived. It was so much better than any place I'd lived so far. I felt like a queen with running water, walls without holes in them, a real bathroom, and even a laundry room.

We pull up to the block where I lived and there, standing under the street light, was Jack. He had his arms crossed over his chest, no shirt on, and looker meaner than a junkyard dog—as usual. The guys freaked out, and I told them to stay calm, let me out, and drive away. I said I wasn't worried about him. Well, that's what they did, and I was glad, because I didn't want my friends to get hurt.

I started toward the door of our apartment, and Jack started yelling at me, calling me a whore, of course. I said nothing and just walked in and continued with my own things I had to do. He hated it when I did that, so I did it all the time. He took a swing, but this time I'm ready.

Remember those fights I used to watch my father fight? I learned a lot watching him, and now I put it into action. Instead of backing up, I stepped toward the Hulk and very quickly delivered a fast and sharp undercut to his chin. I used my full body weight, and sakes alive, I knocked him completely out. The Hulk was on the ground and out! I wanted to do a dance around him, remove his scalp, or something. Instead I took the kids and left; he was going to come to at some point, and I didn't want to be there. I hid out at Marylee's for a couple of days. Jack knew he couldn't get to me there. When he cooled off, the kids and I went home.

So it was back to work. Here's the deal though. After several months on the job, I saw something very different and something I never expected to see. I saw the miracles that nurses and docs do every day—the people they help, the lives they save, the emotions they deal with. I slowly realized that this was something I wanted to be a part of. It must have shown, because a couple of doctors began to ask me to do rounds with them, which I loved because they explained what they were doing and why. I ate it up.

One pathologist asked me if I'd like to see an autopsy. I jumped on this opportunity and loved every second of it. Once we got the details taken care of, I was allowed to go to the autopsy. The patient was a twelve-year-old little girl, which shocked me. I wasn't ready for that at all. I soon got past those concerns, though, because I was mesmerized by the body that I saw and by the comments of the pathologist doing the autopsy.

He could tell, for instance, that the girl was about to ovulate for the first time. I was amazed that anyone could know something like that. He used a lot of Latin terms, and he was very impressed that I knew Latin as well as I did. Knowing Latin made my studies and work much easier. I already knew many medical terms that my peers had to learn.

Dr. Dan Duffy, a general practitioner who everyone loved, took me under his wing for reasons I never learned but much appreciated. He always asked me questions that taught me a great deal. He took me on rounds instead of the nurses. They didn't much like that, but he did it anyway, and I learned so much. He told me I should go to medical school and that he was going to help me. However, once again, tragedy struck. Before he could do anything to help me, he was in a major car wreck from which he subsequently died. We all missed him so much, and I rued the chance I might have had.

Soon after that, Jack got a job in the oil field, though it turned out to be off and on, at best. We moved to a real house in another small town, so I had no job again. He was gone for days on end, leaving me without any resources at all. I still had no radio, no TV, no phone, and no car. So we were hungry again. All my kids and I could do was walk around the town, and that we did. I was beginning to see that Jack wanted me to be without a job and without resources. I just didn't know why.

One day, a huge miracle happened. I was washing dishes at the local Lutheran church and heard an announcement on the radio that the GI Bill was now available to post-Korean War veterans. With a catch in my throat, I realized that meant *me*. The announcement included a phone number to call, and I quickly asked my pastor if I could use his phone for this call (a toll-free number). He was very happy for me and handed me the phone with a huge grin.

Well, the conversation that ensued was the beginning of my new life. Indeed, after all the paperwork was done, I was eligible for money to pay all my tuition, books, fees, and so on for a local registered nurse diploma program. It would also give me a monthly stipend of around $130—close to what I earned working full-time as a nurse's aide, after taxes and everything.

So, there I was—a very young mother of two children under five, with no family support, getting ready to start a very demanding educational program that was heavy with science prerequisites, not to mention long clinical hours. This is when I found out how comprehensive and arduous my high school education actually was. As I plowed through chemistry, biology, microbiology, anatomy, and physiology at the local private college, I hardly studied at all while my classmates were struggling to even pass. I had already learned most of what we had for our first year of college courses. What a blessing that was to me, with my kids to take care of!

I did have to prepare for extensive finals in courses like microbiology and chemistry. We had lab and theory finals. I just loved those courses; they were so interesting that I could have majored in any one of them. One day, as we were getting ready for a microbiology final, I told my classmate and friend, Nellie, that she just needed to relax. "Nellie, you are your own worst enemy! You know this stuff. When you're not being all nervous, you can spit it right out. You know what we're going to do? We're going to have a screwdriver right now—you and me both!"

Nellie jerked her head around to look at me and said, "Oh, that's a great idea: get drunk and go take your micro final. Sure, what a friend you are."

"Nellie, come on. I'm trying to help. We'll just have one drink each—not to be drunk, for heaven's sake—just to relax a little. I'll mix them up!"

So we did just that. The only problem was that, right before we left, after one screwdriver each, I looked at what was left in the pitcher and decided not to waste it. Down it went, and off we went. Nellie was driving—thank God. I still remember getting out of her car at Pramdon University. That's when it hit me, because I wasn't a big drinker in the first place. As I stood up, I realized my legs were wobbly, and I felt like I was in some other place. But I also felt really good—invincible almost.

Nellie was watching me and sarcastically said, "Oh boy, you're going to fall flat on your face!"

"I most certainly am not," I said as we rounded the corner to our classroom. There was Professor Johnson, smiling his gallows smile as all the premed students filed into the room, looking very grim. I, on the other hand, felt remarkably calm and happy. "Bring it on," I quipped to him—and he did. Fifteen pages! It was the War and Peace of final exams. "Holy cow!" I screeched. "We'll never get done with this thing."

Everyone got to work on the exam, and the room was as still as a flag in a windless night. I flew through the exam, finishing way ahead of everyone else. I sashayed up to my professor, and smiling from ear to ear, I laid the exam on his desk as I told him, "I'm done, I'm done," and pranced right out of the room. Not looking back, I didn't see the astonished look on his face that everyone told me about later. No surprise, since I had never acted that way around him and was usually the last person to turn in my exam. I usually reviewed every answer several times—my obsessive- compulsive trait shining though once again. So, the group took bets: I either aced it or I failed it. With my pessimistic slant, I was sure I failed it. But nope, I aced that thing with a perfect score.

I finished all my general education requirements for nursing school with a 3.9 GPA. Feeling pretty smug, I began my actual nursing classes and clinicals. No matter what anyone ever tries to tell you, clinically based.

As a starter, one morning at 0530 (yes, that's 5:30 in the morning!), as I was trying to get my books, clinical supplies and the kids into the van, Sammy, my little boy started screaming his head off. "Just a minute, stop yelling, I'm coming," I snapped at my four year old son. I whirled around the corner into the bedroom he shared with Sally (now five) and saw him sitting on the side of his bed in his underwear, tears pouring from his eyes.

"Mommy, I don't want to get up or get dressed," he sobbed. I was momentarily thrown off by this pathetic picture but immediately regained my foothold and yelled, "I don't care! Get your clothes on. We're leaving in five minutes!" Nothing could get in my way and delay me, because I would fail clinicals for the day—a zero that couldn't be made up. Get two or three of those, and I might fail the whole course.

"Oh my God, how will I get through this for three years?" I cried as self-pity welled up inside me. A few short weeks before, I had no future, because I had no money for school. Now there I was with my schooling all paid for and a monthly stipend. I should have been dancing in the street—if I had the time!

"In the car, kids—let's move it!" It was still as black as the dead of night as the three of us struggled out the door.

I didn't see that it had snowed during the night, so I missed the ice on the front steps. I hit that ice at full speed with an armful of books and the kids right behind me. I was airborne in a second and fell flat on my back in the snow. The kids started to cry, and I felt like it, too. Instead I got up and found out I could still walk, so I gathered all my stuff again. We got in the van, and I got the kids to the nursery and made it to clinical on time—barely, but still on time.

Our day started at 0615 with the dreaded inspection line. On every clinical day, we all had to line up (eleven of us) and be inspected for several items before we were allowed into the clinical areas. Hair length, fingernails (clean, no polish, and filed short), length of skirt (had to be two inches below the knee), no rings other than a wedding ring, earrings limited to one pair of studs.

Our uniform was a blue pinstripe with a white apron over it, except for Bill, our one male student, who wore white pants and a blue pinstripe top. Our uniforms were checked daily for cleanliness and neatness. Our shoes had to be freshly polished and clean. We had our nursing caps, of course, and they had to be attached just right and clean, too—all except for Bill.

As we stood all in a row every morning, we looked out for each other as best we could. That particular morning, I said to Bill, "Get your hair back out of your eyes before she sees you!" It seemed I had become the mother hen for the group.

Our instructor, Ms. Shepherd, had a keen eye for detail, so she didn't miss a thing. "Ms. Parker," she said, "get those earrings out of your ears. If I see them again, you'll be sent home!" We finally got in line and held out our hands for inspection. "Looking good, students, looking good," smiled Ms. Shepherd. "Let me see your lunch money," she added, and we pulled out our lunch money. Bill didn't have any, and I was shocked to see Ms. Shepherd put a couple of dollars in his hand. She wasn't all bad.

Off to our clinical assignments we went. But first we had preclinical—that's where we got quizzed by our faculty regarding the patients we would take care of that day. What medications were they on and what side effects could happen? What was their diagnosis, their prognosis, their treatment plan, and most of all, our nursing plan of care? Then we began our actual care of the two patients entrusted to us. We were responsible for the total care of those patients, including a bed bath.

As we worked in very cramped areas, things sometimes did not go as planned. Mary, one of my fellow students, was trying to get through the curtains that were pulled around her patient's bed when one of the bobby pins on her cap got caught on the curtain and off came her nursing cap—and her wig. It was so funny we couldn't stop laughing. Boy, that hurt!

It was as funny as the day Bill came around the corner with a bath pan full of water and dumped it right on Ms. Shepherd. And how about the day at lunch when we were so hungry, we scooped some enchiladas we had wrapped in napkins right into our purses, because we had to get back to clinical. That was pretty ugly when we got to it later.

After clinicals, we had post-clinical conference— and then we had classes for the rest of the day. One day the funniest thing happened in class. The faculty for this class was the dean of the school, who had absolutely no sense of humor. I sat in the front row, and I knew I couldn't let myself laugh, or I'd have been in big trouble. Well, she excused herself to go to the bathroom, and when she returned, I saw her coming. She was a huge woman (we had to tie her shoelaces for her when she did clinicals), and the white uniform didn't help matters. Well, on this day, she had managed to get the toilet paper stuck in her underwear, and it was trailing along behind her. I still laugh when I picture her, but we all had to stifle it until we got out of there. Then we howled.

We finished each day around four thirty or five. Of course, we had to study for exams, prepare nursing care plans, and look up meds for the next day's patients. Oh, and we had our families to take care of, too—some more than others. I had no help at all; it was the kids and me together. I made a rule that I stuck to the whole three years: I didn't do any of my schoolwork until the kids were in bed. I spent from five to eight thirty or nine with them doing whatever they needed to do. Then I plowed into my work and usually finished around midnight. Off to bed and up again at five. I had three years of that, and I didn't get summers off either.

My student days were very rewarding; I learned so much. One day in my senior year stands out in my memory. My instructor assigned me to care for a man in his thirties who was terminally ill with pancreatic cancer. This case turned out to be the most valuable lesson I could have learned. He was a local minister, and his wife was holding their brand- new first child. I was so sad just looking at them and didn't have a clue what I should say or do.

I studied all about pancreatic cancer, learning among other things how tender the skin became as the tissues swelled and the skin cracked. What a terrible disease, and why on earth would God let something so awful happen to such a good person, so young with his first little son? *How could God do that?!* I was angry with God again. Every day for almost two weeks, I gave this patient almost all of his nursing care. He was my only patient. Only in retrospect did I come to understand the lesson this man taught me.

Every morning, I bathed him, combed his hair, brushed his teeth, changed his linens. Each day, he asked me to help him kneel at the side of the bed so he could pray. Then, when he couldn't kneel anymore, I helped him sit up in bed to say his prayers. When he couldn't do that anymore, he just prayed where he lay. His wife sat quietly in one of the chairs most of the time, holding their baby. I watched all this every day with great sadness and great anger. How could he keep praying to a God who would do this to him and to his family? I was tortured with that question.

Then, one day, as I bathed him, being very gentle with the washcloth because his skin was swollen and painful even to touch, he said to me, "The Lord said: whatsoever ye do unto others, ye do unto me also." I was so stunned by his words and by the fact that as he was lying there dying, he was ministering to me, I ran from the room and stood in the hallway, sobbing.

It took me many years to comprehend what that young minister did for me. His faith could not be shaken. Witnessing faith like that eventually brought me to the Lord again. Faith like that finally helped me let go of my anger. But it took years. He showed me the miracle and the power of human touch; he helped me experience the connection of two hearts. He also taught me a lesson I could teach others: even when you're dying, you need to be who you are until it's over. He was a minister right up to his own death; he ministered to me even as he died. And that's what most of us want—to be who we are until we're gone.

So, all through my life, I've tried to remember and to teach others that when someone is dying, let them do what they can do that gives them the ability to be who they are for as long as possible. This young pastor taught me valuable lessons, and somehow my instructor knew I needed to be his nurse.

We did our psychiatric nursing clinicals at Mideastern State Hospital in Perry, Kansas, a hospital that was for the criminally insane. Without any experience or previous coursework in that field, we should have *never* been in that place, but we were—along with a psychiatric instructor who was wacko. "Wacko" is a diagnosis that I learned from a psychiatrist friend I knew many years later. It isn't in the Diagnostic and Statistical Manual of Mental Disorders IV!

This crazy woman put our only male student on the acute women's ward for his first assignment. Poor Bill had been raised by his grandmother, was about twenty years old, was a virgin, and she tossed him in that snake pit. When they finally got him out of that ward, all he had left on his body was his underpants and shreds of his undershirt. The instructor was nowhere to be found.

Our dorm was right across from the solitary confinement cells of the worst offenders. Imagine the noises and comments they made about the "cute" student nurses. It was an experience out of hell for most of us.

We also had to eat with the patients in the common dining room. That's where we got to see our instructor and the chief psychiatrist chase each other around the campus. No kidding. They were running at full speed, his tie and white coat flapping in the breeze and her cape like a flag blowing in a strong wind as she sped by the windows with one hand anchoring her pointed nurse's cap to her head. You can't make things like this up! None of us ever figured out if she caught him or not, but watching the race was sadly comical.

Then I got my first patient assignment: a thirty-year male paranoid schizophrenic who was arrested on the streets of some big city for slashing people with a huge butcher knife. He was very powerfully built and good-looking. I was scared to death. My palms were wet with sweat. All the psychiatrist had to say to me was "Don't turn your back on him." Now, how was that supposed to help me?

Initially, I thought I knew nothing about paranoid schizophrenics. I prepared by worrying all night. Of course, looking back, I know that I did know what to do. After all, I lived with a PS most of my life. I ended up spending many days with this patient, and in spite of myself, I learned a great deal about the illness, bolstered by my previous experiences.

My peers struggled more than I did, because they didn't get the appropriate theory and guidance from our instructor. They were pretty much on their own except for the occasional staff person who explained something to them. One of the things I learned that will stay with me forever has to do with the fact that many of the patients I saw in that institution were brilliant people. I can't tell you how many had PhDs. Most were highly educated, and that scared me.

It was hard being there without the right supports and also being so far away from our families. I missed my children badly, having never been away from them even overnight. Others missed their husbands, but I was glad to be away from mine. A couple of my married peers began to date other people. They didn't want to leave their husbands; they were just lonely and horny.

Jeff, one of the docs, was good-looking and my type— kind of Black Irish looking. He knew I liked him, and I was really wowed when he started flirting with me. I was stunned when I let myself begin to flirt back. I said to myself, You're no better than the rest of them.

Then I thought about Sammy and Sally and I just couldn't do it. I explained my thoughts to Jeff and we remained friends which was nice.

Still, I thought my peers were a fascinating group of people. Maryann, for example, was a short, stacked strawberry blonde who just wanted to have fun. She had four kids (lots of fun there!) and was not into being a wife or a mother. While we were at the dorm, she was a wild, fancy-free flower child. Nothing was off limits to her. I kind of admired this free spirit, but I knew I could never be anything like that. The thought nagged me for a little while anyway.

Our psychiatry rotation came to a close. Our final exam was in front of us, and we were, of course, all terrified we'd fail and have to repeat that horrible rotation. I was so sure I'd fail that I didn't even study. Guess what. I made a 99 percent on the standardized national exam. I didn't realize how much I'd learned about psychiatric illness by living with my father. I'd never considered it could help me on a day-by-day basis and help with an exam. Eureka!

Our next clinical rotation was pediatrics, and it was at our home hospital. I knew pediatrics wasn't for me, and I experienced two kinds of problems when doing clinicals on pediatrics. First of all, I thought my children were getting the disease the kids I cared for had. Case in point: I took care of an eleven-year-old girl, Nancy, who was admitted with the flu. She had recovered and was going home. I was the nurse who was getting her paperwork and discharge instructions together so she and her family could get the heck out of the hospital.

I'll always remember the moment when Nancy said to me, "I don't feel so good. I think I'm going to vomit." Well, she started vomiting and didn't quit. I never saw someone retch so hard. The doctor ordered an anti-nausea shot. I got it and administered it to her. I was horrified to see Nancy grow worse before my very eyes and the eyes of her very alarmed parents. Nancy died that afternoon. No one knew why. She was better and ready to go home one minute and dead the next—a child.

I was crying almost as much as her parents, and when I went home that night, I continued to cry and to grieve over the whole thing. Then, later that evening, my son started telling me that he was nauseated. My whole body went into hyperaction at that point. All I could think was that my son had what Nancy had and he was going to die, too—unless I figured out what to do pretty darn quick. I grabbed a big pot, filled it with water, and brought it to a boil. I have no idea why I did that, but that's what I did—instinctively. To this day, I have no idea why. Of course, my son was okay, but I didn't know that at the time.

Second, I couldn't take care of those darling kids with all sorts of awful problems and not cry. And you can't cry as a pediatric nurse! So it sure wasn't going to be where I had my career.

One of the pluses in being on peds was meeting the man who would end up being my second and last husband, Jerry Masters. I knew him already but only as a very important nurse manager and not as a person. As I watched him with the children, I was awed by how they responded to him. He was like a magnet to them, a calming presence that they so much needed. I grew to respect his work with children probably more than I ever respected anything else in my career. Of course, his wife, Maryann, was in my class. She was his polar opposite— uncouth, loud, brassy, clumsy, and didn't relate to patients well at all.

Somehow it was destined that Jerry, Maryann, Jack, and I would end up as friends. We started having dinner at each other's houses and going places together like local dances. I saw a different side of everyone, and I found myself attracted to Jerry. But I didn't want to hurt Maryann. Nothing every came of this flirtation, but we got awfully close.

One night, when we were playing cards as we did many nights, someone (I can't remember who) suggested we play strip poker. So we did. Well, I got down to my underwear and couldn't muster the courage to go any further. "I want to go home," I said to the shock of everyone, mostly my husband. Jack said, "Sit back down here, girl, and keep playing. It's just getting interesting." But I started putting my clothes back on and gathering my stuff. Finally, Jerry said, "I think it's time to call it a night." I was so grateful to him for saying that, I hugged him and kissed him on the mouth. I enjoyed that kiss tremendously and remembered it many times, as I know he did, too. He was so warm and gentle.

Well, we made it—all eleven of us graduated. We didn't realize then what a bond we had formed in those three years; we were like family. Every time we saw or talked to each other for the rest of our lives, it was still like family. We had survived so many things together, things we never would have guessed we could master. We were a real team;

we covered for each other, helped each other, and faced our last community obstacle: the national examinations.

Today these exams are called NCLEX, and they're computerized, so you don't have to wait weeks to find out if you passed. In my day, they were on paper and lasted two whole days. Monitors watched us, and it was a very intimidating environment. Then it took six to eight weeks to find out if you passed. Those were agonizing weeks, to say the least. We were allowed to work as graduate nurses during that time (thank God, or we would have gone hungry again). Waiting was awful, because your whole future was at stake. If you didn't pass, you couldn't work as an RN, and the past three years had been a complete waste. You were allowed to retest, but that wasn't an option for me. Failure was just unacceptable.

So, about six weeks later, my letter arrived. I was too scared to open it at first; all of us believed we had failed the exams. I knew I had to open it, and I finally mustered the courage to do so. Eureka! I passed and with a perfect score in psych. I didn't even study for that part because I hated it. I realized that I learned a lot about psych just living with my father—a plus I hadn't counted on!

CHAPTER 5

I'M AN RN!

It was the coolest thing to wear my white uniform, white hose, white shoes, nursing school pin, and most of all, my nursing cap with its wide black stripe, symbolic of the registered nurse. Everyone commented on how good I looked in white with my almost-black hair and dark eyes. I was so proud, and my kids were, too. I will always remember six- year-old Sam saying at our graduation ceremony, "Mommy, now we will never be hungry again." Some of the guests shed a few tears over that comment.

He was right, and that's what we celebrated together, my two children and I. We had it made.

It was fascinating to me that Sam was a charmer even then. After supper every day, he kissed me on the back of my neck and said, "Mommy, that was the best supper I ever had!" Mind you, it might have been a grilled-cheese sandwich. At bedtime after our prayers, as I turned off the light, I would hear his tiny voice say, "Mommy, you're the sunshine of my life!" How can you beat that?

My first job as a registered nurse was in a medium-sized obstetrical unit. I was the only RN on duty on the three-to-eleven shift. I had done my senior leadership project in school on that floor, so I felt pretty secure working there. And I loved working with moms and their babies. My supervisor was Sister Mary Kay, who had worked in OB all her life and was an expert. She expected the same expertise from me, and I didn't have it. This was a bone of contention between us.

A new OB/GYN, (Obstetrics/Gynecology) Dr. Silverton, had a first-time mom in labor and was watching over her. Late that night, the doctor told me her patient was ready to go to the delivery room. I assisted in getting that done, and there we were, this young, new OB doctor and me, the young, inexperienced nurse. And the woman was having twins.

I scurried around getting supplies and staff ready for two babies. The first one was born without problems, and we were waiting for the second when the doctor said, "It's in the birth canal. I just can't reach it." It had now been at least thirty minutes, and even I knew that wasn't good. I left the room and called my supervisor, who assured me everything was fine.

When I went back into the room, the doctor was reading a textbook. Horrified, I thought, *Oh, no, she doesn't know what to do!* I tried hard not to let the mother see how scared I was. I interrupted the doctor, saying, "I can call one of the other OBs for you, Doctor. Which one do you want me to call?" She told me not to call any of them because she'd get this taken care of.

The second baby was born about forty minutes after he entered the birth canal. His cry was delayed, weak, and very shrill. He was very listless. I didn't know what the prognosis was but learned later that he had sustained brain damage as a result of what happened. This haunted me for years. I would see the family all over town, and the mother would always introduce me to her kids and say I was there to help with the delivery. I would cringe every time, because I felt I hadn't done the right thing. I hadn't reacted quickly enough, and I listened to the authorities around me. Today I know that I would have gotten an experienced OB in there stat, no matter what anyone said.

My sojourn on OB was a ton of responsibility because I supervised the nursery, including sick babies with tube feedings, a twenty-bed postpartum unit with surgical patients on it, *and* the six-bed labor-and-delivery (L&D) unit. Yes, it was just me, one RN, and three nurse aides). I told my supervisor, Sister Mary Kay, that I felt this was inadequate staffing, and she told me that's all the staff there was. So I was often there until midnight and usually didn't even "open" my charts until then. I got chastised for not being efficient. You can see where this is going.

One morning as I was going off duty and Sister was coming on, the elevator door opened, and out she swirled in her white uniform and veil. "Hartle," she promptly said when she saw me, "your shoes need polishing!" After the night I'd had, I snapped and told her, "If I were a nun like you, my clothes would all be done for me, my shoes polished, and my meals all prepared and dishes washed. But I'm not a nun, and I have to do all that myself besides take care of my two children—something you know nothing about. So lay off!"

You know what? She did lay off. She never jumped me about anything after that event. Go figure!

But my trials on OB weren't over. It was another evening shift, it was after midnight, and the eleven-to-seven shift RN was on duty. I was officially off-duty but had just opened my charts for the night. My notes were still in my pocket. I was calmly sitting at the nurses' desk, writing out my notes for twenty-some patients when I heard a blood-curdling yell from the L&D unit. In retrospect, I should have ignored it or just gone home, but I didn't. I jumped up and ran back to the L&D rooms, where I knew a multip (a mother who had given birth before) was in labor, and it was a premature labor. (I had told the oncoming RN that she'd better check the patient soon, because she was going to go fast.) This patient was also the wife of one of our pediatricians.

I ran into the room to find her delivering in her bed (a no-no), and her OB, Dr. Pat Simpson, standing there yelling at the top of his lungs. He was a big man, and he was drunk. He grabbed me, yelling, "Why didn't you watch this patient," as he literally lifted me up and tossed my whole body against the wall.

I fell to the floor and looked up at him as he drew back his fist to hit me. Then the patient called out, "No, Pat, don't hit her! It's not her fault!" Yes, the patient who was delivering her premature baby intervened for me to keep this nut from hitting me. I got up from the floor and helped with her care. When I was done, you bet I went hunting for that nurse and found her asleep in the nurses' lounge. I sure let her know what I thought of her behavior.

The next day, I reported both the doctor and the nurse to my supervisor. Sister Mary Kay quickly told me that there was nothing she could do, because the hospital needs docs, and she didn't want to discipline the nurse because she was her only full-time night RN.

My back was sore the next few days, and I found out that when he threw me against the wall, the force had snapped my thoracic spine, but it wasn't displaced. That doc actually broke my back! (This was the same spot where my husband had broken my back a few years before.) Color me stupid, but I never even thought of suing that doc. Can you believe that? Needless to say, I left that position, especially after Sister Mary Kay's comments.

As nurses know, there are always jobs available. I didn't have to lose one day's pay as it turned out. I went from OB one day to the emergency department (ED) the next day. I had one day of orientation, had been out of school about three years, and was scared to death to be the RN in charge of the ED. For a long time, as I walked across the parking lot bridge, I always, always said this prayer: "Please, God, don't let me kill anyone today."

In spite of that gut-gripping fear, this began the love affair of my life. Working in the ED was the greatest, most exciting job anyone could ever imagine. And talk about making a difference in people's lives—wow! For the next several years, I lived the dream: going to work every day, loving what I did, and believing that my work was important. These were the days when there were no doctors in the ED—just RNs and staff. It was a grand experience, because I got to do things I would never have been able to do on a regular floor. I removed casts, ordered x-rays, read them, and applied casts. I was very strong in orthopedics, which was great because it was a trauma hospital.

And then one day, completely out of the blue, I looked up from the registration desk one busy evening and was stunned to see Johnny standing there. I thought I was dreaming, but I wasn't. It was Johnny in his army uniform. I called out to the aide on duty that I was taking a break, and Johnny and I went into an empty room to talk. "Johnny," I cried, "thank God you made it through that horrible war. Are you out now?" I was surprised to feel tears on my cheeks.

"Ahh, Chicky, no tears. I made it, and it's so good to see you. Look at you now—you have a uniform, too." Then he added in a whisper, "Only your uniform is about helping people and mine is about killing people." It seemed so natural to slip into his arms, and we danced slowly around the room, all the while Johnny stroking my hair.

"Chicky, can you come with me?"

"Oh, Johnny, I want to be gone from my husband so badly I can't stand it. But my kids—I can't do that to them. They deserve a home with both their parents. It's not their fault that I'm in a miserable mess." Johnny held me tight and whispered beautiful love words to me that no one had ever said to me. I felt like I was in a magical world. Then suddenly there was a sharp rap on the door, and my aide burst into the room, saying, "We have a trauma case. Got to rock and roll."

"Johnny, you're the best. Stay safe. You've made me feel so good, Johnny." I smiled at him and ran from the room. I felt something I didn't completely understand, but it was good.

The ego behind many physicians, especially the specialists, is no secret. One that I will never forget was a guy by the name of Jarvis Janson, an othropod—an orthopedic surgeon—and one of the best. He was senior partner in a six-man operation. His nickname was T. Rex, and he earned it. I loved the guy, but most of my peers were scared to death of him. There are so many stories I could tell you about him, but one is the very best.

It was a very busy day in the ED, which was also an infamous "cast day," when all the people in the whole region who needed a cast changed came into our ED. On top of that, Dr. Janson had some Eagle Scouts with him to observe what he did. This was particularly ominous, because he always behaved horribly when he had an audience.

I was as busy as you can imagine as the only RN on duty when I heard what I describe as the T. Rex tail slamming against the floor as His Eminence decided to come out of his office to do whatever. It seemed like the floor actually shook with each slam of that imaginary tail. Boom, boom, boom—here he came. I braced myself for the onslaught as he rounded the corner and looked straight at me. "Hartle, call surgery, and tell Merrill I said to get his ass down here and help us," he bellowed.

No, that wasn't smoke coming from his nostrils, I told myself as I reached for the phone. The OR secretary answered, and I asked for Dr. Merrill but was told he was in a case. "Is it a joint replacement?" I asked.

"No, a carpal tunnel."

"Okay, have someone put the phone to his ear."

A minute or two later, Dr. Merrill said, "What's up, Hartle."

"Dr. Merrill," I said, "I am going to quote Dr. Janson, who asked me to tell you to get your ass down here to the ED right now." I waited for the reply to scorch my ear, but what I heard instead made me laugh inside. "Hartle, you tell Janson that I said I'm up to my asshole with cases up here, and consequently my ass won't be coming down there!" I could hardly contain myself as I said, "Dr. Merrill, I'll be glad to deliver your message verbatim!" I hung up the phone and turned to find our infamous orthopod and his two Eagle Scouts, whose eyes were wide with shock, fear, you name it. "Dr. Janson, sir," I said with a grin, "Dr. Merrill told me to tell you that he is up to his asshole in cases upstairs and therefore he won't be coming down here to help us—sir."

T. Rex puffed all up and began his tirade. "That sumbitch—wait till I get a hold of him." He reached for the phone and called the OR himself. Things got worse quickly when he was told that Dr. Merrill refused his call. Egads, we're in for it now, I thought, only to see the phone ripped right out of the wall and smashed with great vigor on the floor.

When I calmly said, "Well, that's one less phone I have to deal with," everyone roared with laughter, including the patients who saw it happen (except T. Rex).

The ED operated with protocols that were developed by various physician groups and administration, and we followed those to a tee. We also had a great on-call system for all our physicians, who always responded very quickly, at least by phone. I think we did as good a job and at a lesser cost as is done now. I always had a complete history and physical on the patient before I called the attending or on-call physician. It was a very thorough approach that didn't rely on expensive testing like you see today. I worked mostly the three-to-eleven shift but often pulled a sixteen- hour shift.

Places like EDs have unusually high levels of stress, and when that happens, you see the staff do things they wouldn't do elsewhere—like having sex at work and saying things that sound terribly insensitive, like "the old guy should just die." While never appropriate, it is understandable. Until you see the narrow thread between life and death every day, you have no idea. We also had huge parties for just about any occasion. There was a tight bond between the Emergency Medical Technicians (EMTs), the ED RNs, and the docs as well. We worked in the shadow of death every day and lost too many that died too early or in really bad ways.

One day when I was working the day shift, I looked out the window just in time to see two men get out of a pickup truck who were obviously badly burned. As it turned out, the local refinery had exploded. They had third-degree burns over a lot of their bodies, and some of their clothing had melted right into their skin. They had gotten themselves to the ED, walked in, and talked to us like it was a routine visit. I was totally shocked (and they were, too).

We got them into our treatment rooms, and I gave them morphine IV before we began the horrible and tedious process of getting clothing out of burns. You never forget those images and smells. I hated to treat burn patients because I felt so badly for them.

One day there was a propane explosion in a home. The woman had flipped the switch to turn the lights on in her trailer, and the whole thing blew up. She and her two-year- old son were badly burned. I cared for them in our ICCU because they needed extra help. It was years before I was able to go to sleep and not hear the little boy cry, "Mommy, I hot" or "Mommy, I thirsty." He died a couple of days later, and she lost the fingers on one hand but lived. I haven't allowed propane to be used in my homes since then. It was such a horrible way to die for that little boy and terrible for his mother to have to hear his cries and suffer the loss of him.

On a funny note, I had a case in the ED one night that I still laugh about. This guy in his forties walked in the door with a bloody towel wrapped around his penis. I got him in a room and began the usual questions and exam. I removed the towel to find a very thin paintbrush handle inserted into his urethra, which was bleeding profusely. He had all kinds of stories for how that paintbrush got in there, none of which made any sense.

I was trying to assess the status of the bleeding along with his vital signs while struggling not to laugh. When I had all that done, the fun began for me. It was about two in the morning, and I was going to have to call the on-call urologist. So I dialed the number, and the doc on call—one of the five-member urology group— answered the phone. I said, "Dr. Soleman, this is Hartle at St. Teresa's ED. It's 2 AM, Saturday, the fifteenth of

October, and I am calling you because you are the lucky urologist on call." I then told him the patient's vital signs and exam data, ending with his chief complaint, which was a paintbrush handle being stuck in his urethra. Trying to keep the laughter under control, I told him I would be glad to call out the surgery team, because this guy would definitely need some anesthesia to get that handle out of there and because I couldn't tell what kind of damage he may have.

We talked about that case for years and laughed every time. I can't tell you how many times I had to dig various items out of vaginas, but I never encountered anything inserted in a male urethra before or since.

One case stands out in my mind because of the lessons I learned from it. This story is about a very pleasant 75 year old lady who sustained a broken back in an MVA (moving vehicle accident). In those days (back in the 70s), we kept patients like her in the hospital while we did various treatments – not that way today. Anyhow, she had to have her body cast changed every so often and today was the day. I knew her from previous visits to the ED so we chatted comfortably as we set about changing her cast. However, before she came down to the ED from her inpatient bed, I had a bit of an argument with the two orthopods who were going to change the cast. They wanted to use the new cast table and I didn't. I hadn't been trained to use it yet and wasn't comfortable with it. I told them that. "Hartle", Dr. Fish said, "we know how to use it". "Well", I said, "I would still feel better using the one I know how to use". Fish turned back to me, "get that new table ready, Hartle! Now!"

Out the door I went to get the dratted table set up but I stopped long enough to call the supervisor. I told her the whole story and she said, "if they know how to use it, go ahead and use it".

I got the table set up, the patient on it and the docs removed the old cast. Now, a basic scientific premise: wet plaster weights more than dry plaster. On goes the wet plaster around and around this little lady's body. The docs are done and I turn to the instrument table to get the scalpel for Dr. Fish to cut the plastic and we're done! In the brief second that my back was turned, I heard a ripping sound and then the sickening sound of bone hitting concrete. I whirled around to see my patient, unconscious with her head on the floor while the rest of her body dangled from one end of the table. Dr. Fish was gagging in the sink and Dr. Johnson was rubbing his hands together, clearly distraught. I called for the orderly to help me get the poor lady off the floor. We took her to x-ray and, of course, she now had a fractured skull to go with her broken back!

The family wanted to sue, of course. But ....the patient said 'no'. She did not want to sue and the reason was that she liked that little nurse in the ED and would not sue her! Wow and wow! She knew that I cared for her as a result of all the conversations we had had during her treatments. As I have told many nursing students, the moral of this story is twofold: when you gut tells you not to do something, don't do it no matter what! Just say "NO'! For years, every time I saw those two docs, they always said 'whatever table you want Hartle". The other lesson is rapport. When you build a rapport with patients, you have a better chance if something goes wrong. Now, that's now WHY you build rapport with patients but it's a nice side effect!

We had many unforgettable events, including things you have nightmares about, things that make you change how you and your family do things (like riding in a car with your arm out the window—if you do that, you've never seen an arm ripped out of its socket). One thing that you don't learn in nursing school or medical school is how to handle all the things you see. I'm here to tell you, after a few years (or less) of that, it takes its toll. You become calloused—or as we called it, jaded—or you get sick or you do wild things— living on the edge because every day is a gift that could be gone tonight.

One night I was alone in one of our big trauma rooms, cleaning orthopedic needles (large needles, three to four inches long). I heard something behind me and turned around to find a young guy in jeans and a hooded sweatshirt with a knife in his hand. He said, "Give me your narcs, or I'll cut you."

I have no idea on earth why I did what I did, because we were all trained to just open the narcotics cabinet and give people whatever they wanted so staff wouldn't get hurt. I never believed that people like this guy would just take the drugs and run. I always thought they would still hurt you or kill you. Anyhow, I looked at the guy, held out that needle, and said, "Make your move, but I bet I can put this needle where it will hurt like hell before you get to me."

Without another word, he turned and ran out of the ED. I reported the incident to my supervisor, feeling pretty proud of myself, and was chewed out for not following policy. Of course, right?

One day I was on duty in the ED, and things were relatively calm. I looked out the window to see a huge guy (tall, not fat) being escorted in cuffs by two cops. They had left the doctors' office next to the hospital and were heading straight for the ED. Then I saw why: he was bleeding profusely from both wrists. Any time you see something like that, it isn't going to be good—and it wasn't.

He had been a patient in the orthopedics office and got mad because he had to wait too long, so he broke out the windows in the office—ergo the blood. He had actually cut some fairly good-sized veins. Problem was, he was whacked out on something. Another lesson: stay away from people who are whacked out, because they have the strength of a bull. This guy, with his arms cuffed in front, practically killed two cops, two EMTS, and me. I saw him actually move a surgical table that was locked in place. I never saw or thought I'd see anything like that.

That was when I hit the panic button. I was trying to get as much sodium amytal into him as I could—anywhere I could. I had given up pretty quickly on trying to get it into a vein. The trauma room looked like an animal had been butchered in there. I was sliding in blood as I tried to stick him with more amytal.

Then the worst happened: his fist somehow connected with my jaw, and I went flying through the air. I landed in a heap on the floor on the opposite side of the room. I lay there—blood everywhere—and wondered where in the heck my help was. Then, all of a sudden, he went down. The amytal had caught up with him—finally!

Now, with blood all over me and a sore jaw, I had to get his wounds sutured, the place cleaned up, and then move on to the next case. At that moment, one of the cops said, "I quit. I can't do this stuff every day." It was his first day on the job, and I didn't know it—not that I could have done anything about it. He took off his badge and gave everything, including his gun, to his partner. "I quit," he said again. "You people are crazy." And out the door he went. Maybe we were.

Well, remember the sex part in the medical field. Almost all of us lived it. I remember a doc who was just gorgeous. Now, I was never a looker—remember Zipper—but I had a good body, and people said my eyes and mouth were alluring. So he did look my way, and we began to flirt with each other at work and to go to bars after work. He wasn't married, but I was. And I'll be darned, I never could manage to do it. Always at the last moment, I saw my kids in my mind, and I couldn't. It was a dud.

Then there were all the real affairs the docs were having, and they would tell me to lie about where they were when their wives called. One of the wives would even come to the ED, looking for her husband. He'd be in hiding in one of the treatment rooms, and I'd tell her he wasn't there. I didn't feel good about it, but I didn't see how I could get out of it and not piss the docs off.

On one night shift, I went to get some supplies from one of the treatment rooms, and when I opened the door, I switched on the lights. There, on the floor, was one of our surgeons with a ward clerk on top of him. Both of them were stark naked, and she had the biggest breasts I ever seen. All I saw in my nightmares were those breasts bouncing up and down. Well, those two didn't miss a beat, and I turned off the lights and closed the door. The only trouble I had was not being embarrassed when I saw them the next time. They had no difficulty at all. It was the seventies!

Well, my turn was coming. There was this male nurse, an Irish guy that I thought was perfect. He wasn't married, and we flirted with each other for months before we actually went out. We were an item for years—right through my divorce and up to my second marriage. I fell head over heels in love with Charles. Amazingly, he loved me just the same. He had the most beautiful black hair, hazel eyes and soft smile.

What went wrong? Why didn't I marry him after my divorce? Well, he was gay! He tried hard not to be, but in the end, it just didn't work. Long story short, he got AIDS and died after a very painful period of time. I went to see him almost every day, and one day when I put my hand on his swollen arm, he opened his eyes and told me, "When you touch me, I want to live." I cursed life up and down those days and cried for days when he died. As Charles wished, I said the graveside elegy: "Do not stand at my graveside and weep, for I am not there. I am in the wind,". That was one of the hardest things I ever did. Charles had been like my soulmate.

Back to work! At another cast clinic in the ED, we had a great lunch prepared by the doctors' wives, and we were really looking forward to it. I was zooming through the ED like a running back to take care of everyone that needed whatever. I had to deal with a gunshot wound, a stabbing, the usual assortment of complaints, and all the cast people.

Our ED was built like a small square inside a large square, and I spent most of my time running around the square.

So I came running full tilt (never a good idea), and my foot came in contact with something my eyes didn't see: a cucumber peel. I was airborne and then, as gravity took over, I fell with a thud flat on my back. The wind was knocked out of me, and I just lay there. I didn't know if something was broken or not.

The funny part was the patient who saw it happen and called out, "Oh no, the nurse is hurt!" Everyone came running, and I just lay there looking up at all of them. Dr. Clark, another orthopod (and a handsome devil to boot), said, "Hartle, I think that was about a seven on the Richter scale," as he reached down to help me up.

"Don't you touch me," I screeched. "Don't even put a finger on me. I'll get myself up." Which, of course, I did and got back to work. Another day, another dollar, right?

My career journey took another turn when I decided to leave the ED and work in public health. I had burned out in the ED and needed something different. However, that choice was the not best I could have made. I went from the ED, where I saw all the trauma and all the things we do to each other, to field work in public health, where I was actually on scene for the same things. In the ED, we cleaned everyone up, and usually the EMTs did some of that before they even get to the ED. In the field, we saw things as they were and as they happened. Unknowingly, I had gone from the frying pan into the fire.

In a way, I relived my childhood through the horrible things I saw in the shacks, the streets, the alleys, the tenements, the reservations that I served. Generally, we would get a nuisance call that there was a bad smell in the neighborhood, and we would have to investigate it. One of the first calls I got as a new public health nurse was such a call.

Even though it was against policy, I ended up going out by myself (big mistake) and arrived at the trailer park. Frankly, I could smell the odor before I got out of my car. Something was rotten. Well, what I found left me with nightmares for many years. I knocked on the trailer door, and when it opened, I saw sights that no one should see. My mind's eye remembers spaghetti hanging from the ceiling and grappling with the incongruity of that as my senses took in all the other sights: several small children running in abandon throughout the trailer, dirt and rubbish everywhere.

Then I saw her, the naked woman who answered the door with only a sheet tied around her neck. It was her cape, and she was like Superwoman or something. She shrieked at me and ran toward me. I had no idea what to do, so I ducked as she ran past me and went outside.

I looked in the trailer, and the smell was so bad I wanted to vomit. I really got sick, though, when I saw the reason for the smell. It was a little boy, maybe four, who had string tied around his arm right above the elbow—and his lower arm was rotting. It was gangrenous. I couldn't believe this was happening.

I learned later that the woman, the mother, was a paranoid schizophrenic whose husband was in the air force but was gone on temporary duty elsewhere. He had left her alone with the kids and hadn't told anyone how sick she was. The whole system had failed. The little boy's arm was amputated. So began my career in public health. I was never going to be the same again.

My next call was a smell report again. When I got to the address I was given, I found a place called the Gourmet Restaurant. You could smell the odor even outside. Inside, all I found was several dark stains in the ceiling tiles—not so unusual. But a couple of these stains appeared to be wet, so I asked what was up above. The cook told me there were apartments over the restaurant.

As I said earlier, policy was that we should go in pairs and I had learned my lesson about that, so I had my partner with me. We went around back, found the stairs, and up we went. When we opened the door, the smell was overpowering. As it turned out, there were five families living up there in five different one-room apartments. I knocked on one of the doors, and when it opened, there stood the biggest man I've ever seen—not fat, just big. He was a Native American, and his face looked just like the face on our nickel. I could barely see light around him, he was so big. I looked over at my partner, and her jaw was hanging down to her neck.

I finally got my voice to work and told the man who we were (although our uniforms clearly told everyone who were). I told him why we were there and asked if we could come in. As he said yes, a little girl appeared between his legs, peering out at us. She was covered in sores, and pus oozed from some of them. Her face around her nose was covered with layers of caked snot, and she was so dirty and smelled so bad, I automatically stepped backward.

But that wasn't the cause of the smell that got reported. As we walked into the room, we saw a mattress in one corner. Other than a couple of table chairs and a small table, there was no furniture but this mattress. I saw something on the mattress and thought it was a small dog. But when I got closer, I saw it was human feces—a lot of it. Some was old and some wasn't. Now we knew the source of the smell.

After a thorough investigation, we learned that all five apartments were the same and that there was no running water in any of them. There was a communal bathroom at the end of the hall, but it was inoperable and had been for months. There were sinks in the apartments, but there was no running water. These people were living like animals. I was incensed, especially when I found out that the apartments were owned and rented by a founding father of our community. He was actually charging these people to live in that horrible environment.

Undaunted, I reported this to the appropriate authorities and got some attention. The owner simply refused to pay for any renovations and just closed the apartments. Consequently, the people living there were very angry with me, because they had no place to live at all. I had made a terrible mistake by letting my own emotions overcome my reasoning. I should have made sure I had alternative housing for them before I called the owner. This was a powerful learning experience for me that I've never forgotten.

I also ran the Family Planning Clinic using protocols from the state's health department. This is a funny story— except for what I said to this woman, which was awful but a result of becoming very jaded and having no mentor to help me learn how I should respond. One thing to know is that the right response is *not* to act like the people you're serving. But that's exactly what we did!

Our policy was to give a six-month supply of birth control pills to the women who came to our clinic after we did all the examinations and education. This was the era when you took the pills for so many days and then you didn't take them for so many days. So as not to confuse our women, we gave each one of them a calendar with big Xs on the days they were supposed to take the pill. Simple enough, right? Wrong!

One day, one of the women in my clinic called me and said she was out of her birth control pills. I pulled her record and saw that I had just given her a six-month supply a month before. My first thought was that she was black marketing them, because I had already experienced that. No, that was not the case, she told me.

I said, "Well, do you have your calendar, and did you take a pill on the days that had Xs on them?"

"No," she said. "I took a pill every time I had sex." When she added, "Is I gonna die?" I sat there shaking my head.

And that's when I said what I shouldn't have said: "I hope so, because you're too stupid to live." That was so wrong, but I said it with no regret at the time. When you see too much that shocks you at any one time and you have no mentor, no teacher, this is what happens. You either leave the job or act like I did—and neither option is good.

It also makes you think about life a lot. You wonder if your life is the best it could be, because it could be over today. A big part of me knew that running around with guys wasn't right. I had brought my kids into the world, and I owned them a good home and a mother. Clearly I was torn between what I knew was right and what I sorely missed.

Before Charles died, we went to lots of places together— most of which were part of business trips. One such evening stands out in my mind like a bright light. I call it "The Case of the Yellow Roses." Charles and I and all of the people on the trip from my organization (about ten) were at a beautiful rotating dining room in St. Louis. We were all dressed to the nines, and I was wearing a floor-length, strapless yellow gown with white trim. I noticed a really good-looking man who had black hair and who was wearing a black tux. He was obviously in charge as he gave orders to the staff to do this or that.

Then I saw him say something to the staff and point at the center of the room. Suddenly all the tables were moved from that area, and before you could blink, a small group of musicians appeared there and started to play. I was really surprised when he walked straight up to my table, reached out his hand to me, and said in French, *"Madame, voulez- vous dancer?"*

Somehow I managed to say, "Mais oui." Up I went, and I danced around and around this fairy-tale room with this very handsome, smooth-dancing man, wondering what on earth was going on. We danced for several songs and then, just as he had appeared, he took me back to my table and said, *"Bonne nuit, madame."*

I was in a state of shock, and the women at my table were absolutely jealous. They thought I'd paid him to come and dance with me. We laughed about it for some time. I never saw the guy again, and I questioned staff repeatedly, but to no avail. No one knew anything about my Romeo.

And, then—then it dawned on me: Charles had done it. Charles knew I spoke French, so I knew he had arranged it. When we were alone, I asked him about it, but he denied it. I asked him over the years, and he always denied it. But I cannot think of any other way it would have happened.

Also, when I went back to my room that night, there were a dozen yellow—yellow—roses in my room. There was no note. What woman doesn't love a romantic mystery like that? It's a beautiful thought I let my mind think about whenever I need to remember something magical and uplifting.

Those memories helped when I had to face things that were anything but pleasant, such as a call from a doc on the local hospital's orthopedic service about a patient he wanted us to see in the home. After hearing the story, I decided that I needed to see this patient myself. My nurses didn't have the experience for that kind of case. This was a young man in his thirties with four children, all five and under. They lived in a reasonably decent home, but it was very small. The patient was an electric company lineman and had been electrocuted on the job. As a result of his injury, he lost both arms and both legs. Yeah, he survived the jolt but wound up like that. Can you imagine? We had to dress the wounds daily and begin the rehab process.

It's almost impossible to describe the horrors that family and I lived through. He begged me every day to kill him. He cried and sobbed about how his family had lost the husband and father they had. The children, as young as they were, became subdued and withdrawn. His wife, so young and pretty, became psychotic and deranged.

I will never be able to forget one afternoon as I worked on my patient's wounds. I heard an unnatural shriek behind me and turned to see his wife coming toward me, screaming and brandishing a huge butcher knife in the air. In my best military voice, I said, "Put it down, Sally. Put the knife down." I repeated that, looking straight into her eyes as she came closer and closer. She looked completely crazed. I had nowhere to go; I was trapped with the closest exit behind her, not me. (That was a lesson I never forgot.) Finally, just when I thought I was a goner and she was going to stab me, she dropped the knife and collapsed in my arms.

How do you ever get over things like that? I don't think we do. Years later, I found myself teaching my students to be sure they always had an exit they could get to, if needed. My adventures in nursing were punctuated by distress calls from my mother back in Ohio. Remember, she's still with my schizophrenic father. Mom would call and say she thought Dad was going to kill her or that he was doing bad things in the neighborhood. One day, she called and said, "Susan, your father is in Mercy, and he almost killed a nurse. You have to come home."

"Mom, what's going on?" I'd always say, and she'd go through the litany of events that led up to whatever was happening. In this case, Dad got appendicitis and wouldn't go to the doctor. Being the paranoid schizo he was, he didn't trust any of them. Well, he got peritonitis and became very ill, as these patients do, winding up in the ICU. I flew home this time because of the urgency.

Usually I loaded the kids and drove the twenty-four hours it took to get there, stopping only for bathroom breaks, food, and gas.

I arrived at the hospital, asked for the head nurse, and introduced myself. She was very professional and understanding as she told me what my father did. Apparently when one of the staff nurses went into Dad's room to hang IV antibiotics, he kicked her in the head so badly she lost consciousness.

When I got there, he was in five-way leathers. The moment he saw me, he hissed at me, "Susan, get me out of here now. They're trying to kill me."

"Dad, quit it right now. I'm not listening to you, and your games don't work on me anymore. So, if you're going to act like you did with that nurse, you're going to stay in restraints. You almost killed that nurse, Dad, and she was only trying to help you get better. So just quit. I don't want to make it bad on you, but that's the way it's going to be!" I stared straight at him, and he knew I meant business. I had learned a lot from being with my dad, and now he was learning a lot from me, particularly how tough I could be. I was my father's daughter after all.

The nursing staff was very grateful that I intervened, and considering what Dad did to one of them, they treated him very well until we could take him home. I found out why the whole thing happened later and was really angry with my mother. It turns out that she didn't tell the staff that Dad was a paranoid schizo. She knew she should always do that, but she chose not to tell them—and that nurse paid the price.

Another sad note during that trip home was when I called Johnny to see how he was, and I found out he was married. We met at our favorite spot from years ago, the A & W drive-in on Twelfth Street (amazing that it was still there). Johnny told me about his marriage to Audrey, whom I knew in high school and was now jealous of. She married my Johnny. I knew I had no right to feel that way and told Johnny so, along with my wish for his happiness.

When I started to leave, Johnny grabbed my arm and spun me around so that I ended up against his chest. He kissed me then—the first time. How bittersweet it was. I clung to him and softly cried. He said, "Chicky, chicky, I will always love you. You go now. We both have to live up to commitments we've made." He was right, but I didn't want to go. But, as always, I thought of my two kids and knew it was the right thing to do.

I walked away and turned back to look at Johnny. He was standing there, his head cocked that certain way with that soft smile that I loved. *Good-bye, Johnny,* my heart said as I walked away. God, between Johnny and Charles, it seemed like I wasn't supposed to have someone to love and someone who loved me, too. I was feeling pretty sorry for myself and had the tears to prove it.

I was back home again and back to work as a public health nurse. It was a mind-blowing experience where I really learned what people can do to other people and where my tough childhood helped me deal with some horrible sights, sounds, and smells. Yet I still had nightmares for years.

To anyone who wants to be a nurse, find a good mentor before you start clinical work. Nurses need debriefing more than they realize. We go from one traumatizing event to another, thinking we're fine when we aren't. It has a cumulative effect, this work that nurses do, and we need to talk each one out with a good mentor before it takes its toll and we burn out or become terribly jaded, as I did, or leave the profession entirely.

As I made rounds in my car one day in February, with the usual biting cold winds blowing across plains and this town I lived in, I drove past a shack and saw the usual broken-down couch sitting on the porch with what appeared to be a diaper-clad doll lying on it. I slowly drove by the house, but as I passed it, out of the corner of my eye, I thought I saw the doll move.

I pulled my car over and headed toward the porch, dressed in my navy-blue public health uniform. What I saw next has never left my mind. It wasn't a doll. It was a human baby, a baby that was bloated with starvation and had cigarette burns on its arms and legs. It mewed like a kitten as I stood there hardly able to move as my brain tried to assimilate what I was seeing. Clad only in a diaper on that February day, its eyes were sunken in its head. On my God, I thought, how could anyone do this? What kind of person— and my brain turned my thoughts to intense anger as I stormed to the door of this squalid place and pounded on it.

A woman opened the door, and the sights I saw through the door were enough to cause a seasoned nurse like me to vomit. The smell was like an open cesspit. "Is this baby on the couch here yours? Answer me!"

She lowered her head and stammered, "Yes, she is." I could see at least four other small children in the house from where I stood. Anger was pounding in my head, and I was stepping forward to grab her and punch her lights out when the other part of my brain told me not to lose it and to focus on helping that baby.

"Why did you leave the baby outside," I asked her. "She kept crying and crying, and I couldn't stand it anymore," she whispered.

"Your baby needs to go to the hospital. Do I have your permission to get treatment for her?"

"My husband will be mad if the baby is gone. No, you can't take her," she countered.

This is where being with my dad helped me again. I knew exactly what to say to her. "Listen," I said, "if that baby dies, he won't like that, will he? I'm a nurse, and that baby is going to die soon if she doesn't get help."

She started sniveling, and I almost lost it again. I wanted to punch her face in so badly. Then she said, "Go ahead, take her, but you have to bring her home when she's better."

I had absolutely no intention of doing that, but I told her I would and hurried to get the baby in my car. When I picked the baby up off that dirty couch, she grabbed my uniform by the collar and held it so tight I had to pry her little fingers off to get her situated in the car as safely as I could. I went straight to the local hospital ED, the one where I had worked.

The staff were horror-struck when they saw the baby and when they heard that it had happened right here in our town. I asked them to call Dr. Jones, who had been upset when I left the hospital to work in public health. He had said public health wasn't necessary, because the docs took good care of all the kids in town. The jaded nurse that I had become wanted others to see it, too.

Dr. Jones came to the ED in a few minutes, but the baby had already died—in my arms. At least she was warm. With one look, his facial expressions said it all. I just said, "I guess you guys missed one." I felt the tears on my face—I didn't even know I was crying until then. Then I saw the tears on his face and knew we were in this together. We lost that baby, and we all were sickened by it. Her death became my marching orders.

I succeeded, with the testimony of Dr. Jones, to get the other children removed from that home and placed in foster homes. I don't know what happened to the parents, but we did find out that the cigarette burns on that little baby were done by the six-year-old son. He was the oldest and was clearly psychotic. He lived in some inner world but was violent to his siblings. I don't know what happened to him either.

Another case that lived forever in my mind is the Alice Miller story. She's long dead now, but I'll never forget her. Alice was mildly retarded and lived on the streets most of the time. She got pregnant at around sixteen and took the baby home to the man she was living with at the time. The baby was around eight weeks old when I got a referral to go see it because it wasn't thriving.

The first sight I saw when I entered the home was this young girl carrying the baby around the house by one of its feet. I would not have believed this if I hadn't seen it. I gotta tell you, despite all the teaching, demonstrations, and frustrations Alice and I went through, I never got her to carry that baby right.

Well, that wasn't the worst of it. The reason I got the referral was because the baby was starving. The reason— well, you won't believe that either. Alice didn't and couldn't understand how to feed her baby. She dutifully gave the baby her bottle every so often, and the baby would suck hungrily as babies do at first and then slack off a little. Well, when the baby slacked off, Alice was done. Out came the bottle, even if the baby got only half an ounce of milk. And Alice could not learn to do differently, no matter what I did.

I couldn't go to her house every time the baby needed milk, so I decided my only option was to get that baby removed from its mother. I talked to our juvenile officer and medical director, and the wheels were set in motion. They turned very slowly though, and I worried that the baby would die. Well, the courts ruled against us, in essence saying we just needed to do a better job teaching her. That week, the baby died.

I was furious and not fit to be around for days. I guess this is a good place to mention my children and the sad price they paid for my career. First, I forbid any contact with me when I got home until I had gone to the laundry room, stripped my work clothes off, and put them in the washer—along with Clorox. When I was in my regular clothes, my kids and I sat together on the living-room floor and talked about our day.

I would guess that they were probably the best-educated kids in the world—from a street-smart perspective. I told them everything. When they were ten and eleven, they learned about what horrors people do to themselves and each other. They also suffered through my mania about food. I saw such starvation (and as you will remember, I lived through my own starvation times) that I wouldn't let any of us throw away any food. What went on your plate, you ate. No exceptions.

We never went out to eat, because I didn't have that kind of discretionary money. But we had food every day, and that was something I never took for granted. In the back of my mind was always the nagging thought that something would go wrong and we'd be hungry again. Thank God that never happened.

One year I was asked to represent public health nursing at a conference for Catholic hospitals, and I was the only layperson in the group. When I got there, an old nun dressed in the old floor-length habit was registering everyone. Now, these were the times when nuns were leaving the convent or at least not wearing the habit, so she was the only nun in one.

She also couldn't hear; she actually had one of those ear horns up to her ear. She couldn't get my name straight and kept calling me "Sister Mary Susan." I tried to correct her numerous times but finally gave up and took the nametag that said, "Sister Mary Susan," and put it on my dress.

By then, most of the seats were gone, so I had to sit in the front row. I wasn't pleased with all this, and I had no idea what was coming. Suddenly the curtains parted, and out swirled a commanding presence in a scarlet robe and hat—it was the archbishop! He was a hawk of a man and inspired instant fear in me. He looked around the group and had begun his comments when his eyes settled on me. "Oh God," I whispered to myself, "he thinks I'm a nun! My nametag says I'm a nun." Even for the times we were in, I was dressed a little rakishly for a nun: nail polish, makeup, low neckline.

What am I going to do, I thought. I sat there praying he would finish soon so I could get out of there. When he finished, I jumped up to leave the room as fast as I could, but out of the corner of my eye, I saw him start after me. *Egads, what am I going to do now?* I thought as I picked up speed. I saw Sister Mary Clarence, the mother superior, and ran for her, grabbed her by the arms, and swung myself behind her. "Sister Mary Clarence, the archbishop is after me. Help me!"

There he came, looking like he could conquer even the devil himself. "What is going on with this nun?!" he bellowed at Sister Mary Clarence, who with one arm around me said, "Your Eminence, she is with me, and she is not a nun. The registrar made out her nametag incorrectly." Thank God for Sister!

Back to my personal reality. Jack and I still didn't get along, but he was gone most of the time, and I loved that.

He came home from his oil-field work on weekends, and I dreaded those times. When he left for the oil field on Sundays, my heart was glad and my spirit was free. We did have a couple that we socialized with that Jack knew; he and Mark had worked together. So on weekends, we often had dinner (that I cooked) and watched TV or played cards. This was our routine for the years we were together.

It came to a rough and sudden end when I came home from work early one day and found Grace (Mark's wife) in bed with my husband—my own bed in my own house! Did I mention that I paid all the bills for the house and the rent, too? Well, I did, and I was royally pissed at both of them. I lost my temper and chased her out of the house. I think she thought I was going to hurt her, and it was certainly in my mind as I ran her out the door.

Then I told Jack to get out too. He thought I'd cool off later, so he left. You know, I didn't really care what he did with other women, except I didn't want any diseases, and AIDS was everywhere then. I did care, though, that a woman I thought was my friend had betrayed me that way. Well, looking back, it was just another example of the same old thing that has happened through the millennia. Still, though, it stung.

That was the catalyst that brought me to divorce Jack. People all say they don't understand why women stay in an abusive relationship. There are many reasons, including having no place to go (I mean really no place to go, especially if you have small children) and being afraid of being found and beaten even worse (because that's what the abuser tells you over and over). Then there are the kids who want both their parents and who don't want to be from a divorced family like some of their friends. I knew that it would really hurt Sam, because even though his father beat him, he loved him. I guess it was a natural thing compounded by the fact that Jack was gone so much. Anyway, I knew a divorce would really hurt my son, which was the last thing I wanted.

About a week later, Jack and I had another huge fight. He tore up one of my favorite classics, War and Peace, because he wanted me to read the Bible. Yes, this violent man had gotten religion. It made him even more violent, because now it was his God-given right to correct the kids and me, even if it took a little beating here or there. I sat on the floor and just stared. I refused to read the Bible even then. "Just leave me alone", I cried. He was so furious that he pummeled me with his fists. I know I should have read it but I just couldn't allow him to control me. Then he flew out the door to go wherever.

That's when the kids came to me to comfort me, and I will always remember my young son's face with tears streaming down it. "Mom, you have to get a divorce before he kills you," he cried. They both said that over and over, and I naively thought, This is it. They understand that I need to get a divorce, and we will all be okay. Well, we were all okay, but we lived through years of hell first—especially Sam.

The story of my divorce would make the movie The War of the Roses seem like a picnic. It was something no one could even conjure up. It was so much more than I even imagined, even with my pessimistic attitude. We all paid a huge price that no one could predict. Over the years, when friends have asked me if he or she should get a divorce, I've always said, "Try everything else first. Do your best to make it work, even if it's not perfect, because the divorce will tear your family apart for years, if not for good." In the end of it all, we survived and did well, but for years we lived in a greater hell than we did with all the beatings and fights.

I found a lawyer who was a navy vet and seemed to be someone I could talk to. He was married and probably not the busiest lawyer around or the sharpest, but he didn't cost much, and he listened well. We ended up good friends. He filed the divorce and told me what I should and shouldn't do. I don't remember much of that. I do remember Sam sobbing for hours when I told him I had filed and when his father left the house with his personal belongings. (I still can't believe he left when I told him that he had to.)

We spent that first night together, the kids and me, with Sam sobbing, Sally huddled up to me, and Sam and my mother, who was visiting, trying to help with food and stuff like that. I was sick to my stomach because of Sam and because of the unknown. Would Jack come back and beat me? What would I do if he did?

We finally wound up in court, and I had the one judge in the county who did not abide women working and getting divorces. He was so hateful to me that I didn't expect to get my divorce. But then Jack pulled the trick of the decade; it was like watching a sitcom. There we all were in the courtroom, which was filled with people who knew us. (I didn't know that they would even care, much less take time out of their schedules to come to a divorce trial.) Most of them were from the Baptist church we went to and were very critical of me because I was doing this. They even came to my house to tell me I should not divorce Jack because it was a sin to do that, even if he beat me. I showed them the door.

But I digress. We were in the courtroom, and his lawyer asked me something (can't remember what), and when I answered, Jack went berserk. My lawyer and I were seated at a large, oblong wooden table, and Jack and his lawyer—a bigwig in our church—were seated across from us. Well, all of a sudden, Jack sprang from his seat like a jack-in-the-box, jumped across that table, and grabbed me by the throat. The two of us landed on the floor as he choked me.

My lawyer jumped on top of Jack, trying to get him off of me. Of course, that was mission impossible, because my lawyer wasn't much bigger than me. And Jack—well, you know—he was big. People were hollering, and I was getting lightheaded as I saw the judge stand up with his black robe swirling around as he yelled, "Bailiff, arrest this man immediately!" Well, that was music to my ears, and I was delighted when the bailiff and a couple of other guys pulled him off of me.

Long story short, I had bruises on my throat for a while, and the judge awarded me full custody of the kids, saying to Jack, "I wouldn't give you custody of a dog!" This was a major highlight for me and one of the few that I would experience. Of course, they kept him in jail only overnight, so my peace and quiet didn't last for long. I just felt good that the judge and the Baptists saw the other side of my Bible-quoting husband, the one I lived with.

So, I had my divorce, but I wasn't free of him. What a foolish notion that had been! No, he was always there somewhere, watching me, following me, yelling at me, embarrassing me at work. I made every effort to make things work for the kids' benefit. I allowed Sammy to go with his father on weekends even though I didn't have to by the court decree. I was very conscious about not demeaning Jack in front of the kids. He was their father, and they were part of him. Making him a villain only hurt them. I am very thankful that somehow I was able to understand that and do that, because that helped my kids tremendously.

Well, just when you think you're in control and the worst is behind you, look out! We'd had a few weeks without their father badgering me, and we were enjoying the calmness, playing badminton in the yard or card games in the house. It was July 4, 1976, and we were going to a special bicentennial fireworks show with my dear friends, the Townsends. We had a wonderful time at the park with our blankets out and snacks for everyone as the fireworks exploded in a myriad of colors all around us.

Sam, the firebug, really wanted to be behind the scenes lighting the fireworks, not watching them. "Mom, when I grow up, I'm going to be a demolitions guy," he teased.

I laughed with him and said, "Well then, you're going to have to learn how to keep from burning yourself" (an inside family joke). Then we went to Braum's for ice cream, which was the best treat of all. Then it was time to go home and to bed—or so I thought.

We waved goodnight to the Townsends, and I unlocked the kitchen door. The minute I stepped into the kitchen, I was on high alert. I knew something wasn't right. But what? My heart hammered as I pushed the kids behind me and walked through the kitchen into the living room. There I saw all my candles burning. My brain was trying to understand what my eyes were seeing, but it couldn't. I didn't burn the candles at all, much less when no one was home.

The kids and I stood there, transfixed with fear, the gut- knotting kind of fear. A primeval feeling coursed through my veins: someone is trying to hurt my family. I put the candles out, and then my daughter cried out, "Mom, all our fish are dead!" Sure enough, all our beautiful fish were floating on the top of the water. Next to the fish tank was an empty bottle of Clorox. "My God, someone poured Clorox into the fish tank," I cried out.

We went through the rest of the house and found the lights on in almost every room. In my room, another chilling sight. My underwear was all over my bed and cut to shreds. I knew then that I had to call the police, and I did.

I never dreamed how useless and aggravating the police would be. It seemed from the very beginning of their questioning that they believed it was somehow my fault. Who was I dating? Who was I sleeping with? That made me mad, which didn't help. "Officer," I spat, "this isn't because of something I did. I don't even know anyone who would do something like this."

"What about your ex?" the officer asked. "Even he wouldn't do this," I countered.

Then, the other cop did it when he said, "What about your daughter? Who is she sleeping with?"

I lost it completely and yelled, "Get out of my house, now! Get out!"

"We haven't finished our report," he stammered. "Screw your report. Get out! I'm going to file my own report."

I don't know how we slept that night, piled up together in Sally's bed, closer to the phone. (There were no cell phones then.) But we did sleep, thank God. The next day, the kids went to school, and I went to work. I called the police department on my break and asked for a supervisor. A really nice guy took my call, and I explained what had happened at my house the night before and how the officers made me so mad. I told him I didn't want to file a complaint, I just wanted the police to take me seriously and try to help my kids and me.

He was a sergeant, and I knew him from the ED. That helped, and I was glad for it. He made an appointment to see me at my home that evening. Everything he said and did was the opposite of what the cops did the night before. I thanked him profusely and almost cried because someone was actually listening to me. Sergeant Davis told me what to expect and gave me his card to call if anything else happened. He went all through the house and made sure my locks were good. He told me it was probably a kid tormenting people and I wouldn't hear any more of it.

He had no explanation for how someone got in the house with the doors locked. That's why the cops thought it was one of the kids' friends who had somehow gotten a copy of our house key. From the very beginning, all of them thought it was my ex-husband. I told them it wasn't him— that even he wouldn't scare the kids like that. Besides, I had changed the locks when he left. Sergeant Davis left, and the kids and I settled down to our normal routine. But when I look back on it, I really felt a great sense of unease.

It wasn't a week before the real nightmare began. I was sound asleep when the phone rang at two in the morning, and I woke up. I had to go down a flight of stairs to get the phone, and when I said hello, I heard a weird voice, kind of raspy, saying, "Wish I was with you right now." I hung the phone up so hard, it's a wonder it didn't break.

I gasped for breath. My heart rate must have been over one hundred. Amazingly, the kids were both still asleep. I lay awake the rest of the night, trying to figure out whose voice that was. Morning came, and off to school and work we went. Every voice I heard, I strained to hear if it was "the voice." I didn't tell a soul at work, but I did call Sergeant Davis. He told me the call probably had nothing to do with the other incident. He had a calming voice, and I felt better just talking to him.

Well, that night, the phone rang again around three. Same crap, and I hung up again. I called Sergeant Davis as soon as it was daylight and told him that I didn't believe it wasn't connected anymore, and I wanted something done about it. He said he would put a trace on the phone. "Okay, okay," I told him. "That works for me." Well, to make a long story short, this person called me between two and four in the morning for six months before they caught him. I don't know how I lived through it, because I never got enough sleep.

I told Sergeant Davis I couldn't take much more, and then he told me that they finally got him. I was so overjoyed, I didn't even ask any questions, just jumped up and down and cried. Sergeant Davis blew me away with his next comment. "Like we thought, it was a kid, a sixteen-year-old doing this not only to you but to three other women at the same time. One of them is in the hospital with a nervous breakdown. And this kid is a friend of your son." I asked him who the kid was and was told that because he was a minor, he couldn't tell me. I was furious and said so in very terse, loud terms. Didn't do any good. Sergeant Davis hung up, saying, "Now, you can get some sleep. He'll be in custody for a few months."

I slept well that night, and that was great, but I was still troubled. I wanted to know who this kid was. I wanted to know why he was doing this to us. After thinking about that for days, I decided to contact one of the juvenile officers that I knew very well and had worked with on several cases. I said, "I have to know who this is. I won't do anything, I promise. I just need to know so I can actually rest. I have to get the pieces put together, or I'm going to lose it!"

I didn't think she'd tell me, but she did. It turned out to be the sixteen-year-old son of one of our wealthiest families, and he had a rap sheet as long as your arm. He had been in and out of juvenile facilities all over the county. And his brother was my son's best friend. Mystery solved. Of course, he wasn't arrested; his father intervened as usual, and off he went to another psych center. I was just relieved that it was over. I could sleep again. Joy!

So, back to work, back to normality. The kids and I were pretty happy with life in general. We had such a good time together, playing board games and tennis, and going to movies when I could afford it. My ex didn't pay one red cent of his child support, and the last thing I wanted was to go back to court with him and get choked half to death again. So I took care of everything. Sam spent every other weekend with his father, even though the judge said he didn't get that privilege anymore. I wanted my son to know his father, so that's what I did but I hated it when my boy was gone. Sally wouldn't go, no matter what I said, so I let her do that, too.

What a prankster Sam was—duly inherited from my Irish father! He pulled many pranks, but one of the best was when I took him, Sally, and a good friend, Winnie, and her family (who were Mennonites) to see the opening of Butch Cassidy and the Sundance Kid. I had no idea this was the first movie with frontal nudity. When she undid her blouse, you could have heard a pin drop in the theater. And in that silence, my son yelled, "Mom, look at those boobs!" With pure reflex, I slammed my hand over his mouth, but not before the whole theater broke out in laughter and my poor friend sunk down as low in her seat as she could get. None of us will ever forget that day. Winnie, in particular, will never forget it.

Speaking of Winnie, this is as good a time as any to tell her story even though I would rather never think of it again because I acted so badly. Winnie and Art Townsend were dear friends. Winnie was in my class in nursing school. I had a love-hate relationship with Winnie. She was in many ways my best friend and I know she did everything to help me but I was green with jealousy. I told her it wasn't fair that she had so much and I had so little. Winnie had two kids and a great husband, Art. They had all the money they needed and she only worked as a nurse when she wanted to! He adored her and did everything for her. You can see why I felt the way I did at times. On top of all that, Winnie and Art were devout in their Christian faith. Anyone could see that their faith was their story. Neither Art nor Winnie ever preached to me, though. Instead, they were 'quiet lights' in the storm for me.

One day a couple of years after we graduated, I got a phone call from Winnie. She had just been diagnosed with ovarian cancer and was in the hospital waiting for surgery the next day. I went in to see Winnie right away, of course. I wanted to spend some time with her as she faced this scary ordeal. I stayed with her in that private room the night before her 0700 surgery in the morning, just talking about everything. I was amazed at her calmness and before I could shut my mouth, I heard myself say "Well, Winnie, where's your God now?" I wanted to cut my tongue out but Winnie was unperturbed. She simply said that He was there with her and with me, too. All the while, she smiled at me with that Mona Lisa smile – never a cross word or even a scowl at the cruel comment I had made. It was like I was looking at Jesus himself!

Over the years, I came to realize that it was Winnie's quiet faith that brought me back to God. How could it not?

Winnie died six months after that night before her surgery. She was only 33 years old. She had so much but died so young. What a lesson in that!

Back to my kids. We were so close. I love to think back to how we sat on the floor and watched our favorite shows on TV, me in the middle and each of us with our own blanket. It was popcorn, treats, drinks, laughing at Lucille Ball or watching Gunsmoke or Laugh-In. Life was great when we were all together like that. No beatings to worry about, even if we did something wrong.

Sam was full of laughs and tricks. His sock drawer would have any number of dead animals in it for me to find when I put his laundry away. I chased him around the house a number of times over whatever ghastly dead carcass my hand touched! He made me laugh no matter how I felt and I loved him for that.

Then one night the phone rang around two. I came down the stairs to answer it, thinking it was the hospital and I'd have to go to work. But it wasn't. God, no—it was him again. All I could hear was his raspy breathing, but I knew it was him. I slammed the phone down and went berserk, I think. I ran through the house, trying to think: What should I do? Oh god, I can't go through all that again. I can't. Finally I collected myself and the kids. (Yes, the phone woke them up, too, because of what we had lived through before.) We were in Sally's bedroom, and we talked about the whole thing. I had to be calm for them, and that helped.

I got my wits about me and found Sergeant Davis's phone number. I waited until a reasonable hour and called him. I found out that this psycho teenager was out of the psych center, that they could keep him only so long, no matter what. I just wanted to cry, because I could see that the cops couldn't do much and that the kids and I were victims again. He would call and drive us nuts until he got tired of it or someone complained about him again.

I was heartsick. But we had work and school to contend with, so off we went. That night, I could hardly sleep, and sure enough, the phone rang at the darkest hour of the night, as he knew to do. When I answered this time, what he said turned my blood to ice. "I like the yellow nightgown you're wearing," he hissed as I looked down at what I was wearing.

"Jesus, he can see me," I gasped as the phone fell from my hand. My nightgown was yellow. I didn't tell the kids what he said, because it would have terrify them as it had me. I just sat in my chair, thinking of what to do to stop this nightmare.

After what seemed like hours, a thought popped into my head. I remembered an undercover cop I'd met working in the ED. *That's it*, I told myself. *I' ll call him.* I got his number from the guys at work and called him. Scott came out to my house that morning, because I had decided to stay home to meet with him. We had quite the conversation, and he told me what I should do.

"First of all," he said, "don't call the police. They can't help you. Instead you have to take charge; you have to catch him somehow." I was stunned by this and thought, *I have to face this guy? Me?* But after a few days of work with my newfound skills, I came to terms with that idea, and I was ready to face him. Night after night of his harassment and no relief from the police had brought me around. On top of that, he seemed to be escalating in his tricks, and I was worried for the kids.

Scott taught me that a rolling pin is my best friend. He told me that a gun was no good. I would lose for shooting a minor, even with what he had done and even if he was in the house. So I learned what an effective weapon a rolling pin could be—when used the way Scott taught me.

He also taught me that women make several mistakes when in situations like this. First of all, talking is not the answer and should not be a part of the plan. The element of surprise is a woman's best tool, along with hitting the individual as hard as you can the first time. I'll never forget when he told me that women often hit their attacker and then try to help him or make sure he isn't hurt. He told me to forget all that, hit him as hard as I could, and get the hell out of there. If he died, good. If he didn't, he could still attack me. I have never forgotten that piece of advice, and I've passed it along to others.

So my stalking of this character began. First, when he called, I started telling him he should come over so we could see each other face to face. Surprisingly, after a few nights of saying that, he told me, "You're right. I should come over. You need it, don't you?"

I felt a mixture of nausea and rage as I hung up the phone. Then I spent the rest of the night patrolling the inside of my house, but he didn't turn up. I had already taken the blackout drapes down so I could easily see someone coming up to the house in the dark. Our house was a split-level, and I could follow someone outside by going from window to window.

I don't know how I survived those weeks. Not sleeping much at all, working as usual, getting the kids to all their games and school activities. I don't know how I made it, but I did and we did.

The next night, I waited for him. I sat in a hidden spot in my house. The kids were asleep and the lights were all out as I thought about life in general and how weird things turn out. Suddenly I heard a noise from outside the house, and I knew it was him. It was a scraping noise, one you wouldn't even notice if you weren't straining to hear things. It sounded like someone scraping a shoe on concrete. *The driveway*, I thought, *he's on the driveway!*

I quickly but quietly moved through the house, watching his shadow along the wall of the house next to mine. Then I saw him. My heart hammered. *Yes, that's him*, my brain told me. The adrenaline coursed through my veins, and my focus sharpened. I could sense him, almost feel him like you feel the fog curl through the trees. I felt calm but very alert. I followed him around my house with my rolling pin clutched close to me. He was outside, and I was in. When he came to my daughter's window (she was sound asleep), he shinnied up the brick wall and easily reached the windowsill. I was flattened against the inside wall, watching him push the window up and reach inside then place his hands across the windowsill. It was the very moment I was waiting for, the moment I had planned.

I lifted that rolling pin and brought it down with all my might across the knuckles of both his hands. I heard his bones cracking over his screams of pain, but I hit him again and again. I leaned down and stuck my head part of the way out of the window, grabbed him by his long, dirty blond hair, and pulled his face next to mine as I hissed, "If you ever come back here, I'll rip your throat apart with my bare hands!" I dropped him, and he fell to the ground. As he lay there moaning, I smiled, very satisfied with what I had done. Finally he got up and ran off into the darkness, never to bother my kids or me again. I have never felt a moment of remorse.

Life got better then. Almost normal. We slept all night without those calls. Before long, it was a memory—finally!

As I said, my dear son was the family prankster, so whenever something happened, he was the target. We always knew it was Sam at it again. Well, one year, I blamed him for a particularly ingenuous stunt that both of the kids pulled.

I always left for work before they did, and they came home for lunch but I didn't. However, a couple of my friends worked across the street from my house, so they went to my house for lunch and to check on the kids for me. This was our ritual. I was working as usual and having a peaceful day when the principal of the school called me at work. "Mrs. Hartle," she said, "how are Sally and Sam?"

"How are they?" I asked. "They're fine. They're in school, right?

"No, Mrs. Hartle, they're not, and they haven't been here for two weeks."

My brain couldn't grasp that, and I said, "No, they're there."

Wise woman that she was, she flipped the switch on the intercom and asked both of the kids' teachers how long it had been since the kids were there. They both said it was over two weeks, and they were very concerned and hoped they were getting better.

I just hung up the phone and made a beeline for my car. I sped all the way home, and when I got there, I found the house in the same state as when I'd left it: all the blinds were pulled, all the lights were off, and there wasn't a sound to be heard. I stood there, taking it all in as I yelled, "You two get down here!" Nothing. I started toward the stairs, and then here came our little toy poodles down from the bedroom area. And right after them came my two geniuses, hanging their heads as they came into the living room to face me.

"What on earth do you two think you are doing? Sam, really, this is too much. Your pranks are over." That's when I found out that it wasn't Sam who organized this escapade, but Sally, the one who never did anything wrong. I was stunned. She told me, "It was only going to

126

be for one day, but we couldn't figure out how to get your signature so we could get back into school."

Well, off to school we went. The principal lined the three of us up in a row. I'll never forget what she said. "Sam, you're a Boy Scout. Sally, you're a straight-A student, and Mother, you're a—a—a nurse!"

When the other kids were getting out for spring break, my little darlings stayed in school to make up the time they played hooky. And the whole school system changed its policies so that no one could do that again. If a child was ill, the parent had to inform the school immediately. So we got a new policy for the whole school district—all on account of my kids.

Back to the ex. He was always hanging around, popping up here and there, even at the hospital. I remember thinking, *If that's religion, I don't want any part of it.*

I flashed back to the day he tore up a book I was reading because I didn't want to listen to him harangue me with his biblical quotations. I had nothing against the quotations; it was how he tried to shove them down my throat. He had been a liar and a cheat all the years I knew him. He stole every time he got a chance and wrote checks when he didn't even have a checking account. Then he got religion, and all the rest of us were supposed to, too. That wasn't anything I wanted to be a part of—well, that and a thousand other issues that had led me to the lawyer and away from a really bad marriage.

But even after all that, he just didn't go away. If it weren't for the kids, I'd have moved to the other side of the moon. But they needed their father, and I didn't want to mess up their lives any more than I already had.

So the game continued right up to the phone call I got one evening from a couple we knew at church. Bonnie asked how I was and then told me that Jack had called them. "Susan, he wants to talk to you about the kids, and he asked if you would come over to our house with us there to talk with him."

I made a face and shook my head as she added, "Susan, what would it hurt? We'd be there. He sounds so sad, and really it's about the kids."

Well, you guessed it. I gave in and said I'd go and added, "Bonnie, if you both aren't there, I'll leave the minute I get there. I'm not going to be alone with him."

We set up the meeting for the next evening, and as I pulled into their driveway, I had the uneasy feeling I always had when I saw Jack. It was fear, primal fear. Being near him had spelled disaster for me more times than not. I got out of my car and started to the door, and then Bonnie was at the door, saying, "Come in, Susan. Jack's here."

Bonnie's husband, Bill, was talking to Jack when I walked into the living room. Jack looked at me, and I saw anger in his eyes—an omen of what was to come. He started yammering at me about what I had done to the family. "I told you a divorce would divide us, and it has. We're not a family anymore."

"Jack, we were never a family," I said. "So, what did you want to talk about? I thought it was about the kids."

He just kept lecturing me as if I hadn't said a word, so I turned and walked out the door. That's when I noticed that Bill was gone. *Where in the hell did he go?* I thought as

I headed for my car. *He promised he'd be here in case there was trouble. I just need to get out of here.*

Well, I didn't make it to my car. The next thing I knew, Jack was choking me. I drew back and socked him in the eye as hard as I could. He still held me by my throat and was banging my head on the vehicle in the driveway. I was gasping for air and hitting him as hard as I could when I saw Bonnie out of the corner of my eye. "Call the police, call the police," I croaked as Jack continued to choke me and rap my head against that car.

At some point, he dragged me along the driveway by my hair, and I truly thought he was going to kill me. I couldn't break free, and no one was coming to help me. I kept fighting back; it was all I knew to do. I know I landed some pretty good punches but nowhere near what he did to me.

Finally, when I was close to passing out, I saw the lights of the police car headed toward us. *Thank God,* I thought. *Thank God. I can't hang on anymore.* I wasn't crying; I never cried when he beat me. I wouldn't let myself show weakness to him.

Jack let me go when he saw the cops coming. I stood up and was surprised at the blood running down my leg. The two cops went to Jack—not even one of them came over to see if I was okay. Then I heard the most amazing thing I've ever heard before or since when Jack said to them, "She hit me first!"

Now, keep in mind that he's six two and I'm five four. Even if I had hit him first, it wouldn't have mattered. Those cops didn't take a statement from me at all. They didn't call for medical attention for me, which I learned later that I needed. No, they wrote down what he said and left.

I was angry at Jack, at my friends, and at the cops. How could something like this happen? *How could they not even ask me my side of the story?* I knew most of the cops in town from my work but had never seen those two before.

I got home and hurried to my room, because I didn't want the kids to know what happened. My throat was all bruised—to the point of being able to see part of his fingerprints. But, worse than that, my left leg was bleeding from the thigh down to the calf, because I had basically lost the first layer of skin when he dragged me over the driveway.

I found pajamas that covered all that and went down to be with the kids. I was worried Jack would follow me home, but he didn't. When the kids were in bed, I checked out my wounds again, and they looked even worse. I made myself scrub my skinned leg with soap, like we did in the ED. I didn't want an infection, but boy, that burned. I wondered how on earth I would work the next day. And I didn't want anyone to know about this. I searched through my work clothes to find uniform pieces that would cover my neck and my legs.

I was in such a state of shock and trauma that I didn't even think of what my brain well knew. I should have gone to the ED so I could be treated, because my leg was going to swell as a result of the debridement of my skin on the driveway. It never got to my conscious level. I also had no idea then that the head beating that I took injured my eighth cranial nerve and that, in a couple of months, symptoms would appear that I'd have to live with the rest of my life.

The next morning when I woke up, the first thing I felt was that my left leg was tight, and it hurt to move it. I looked down at it and was shocked to see how swollen it was. My left thigh was as big as my waist. I was horrified. How was I going to work when my leg hurt so much? Well, I just had to. My neck was a darker purple than the night before, and I could still see his fingerprints in places. God, I was a wreck.

I made myself get dressed, and the more I moved, the better my leg began to feel. Then I went to work and began my shift in the ED. Soon my thoughts were dedicated to my patients and their needs, which was what I wanted. What I didn't know is that others around observed things very well—trained clinicians that they were. So they picked up that I was limping and asked what was wrong. "Oh, just hurt my knee. No problem," I told them.

That worked for everyone except one doc who knew me well. He said, "Hartle, I know something is wrong with you, and it isn't just your knee. I can see your neck is all bruised. So, what's going on?" I told him and asked him not to tell everyone else there. He wanted to see my leg and neck, and so I showed him. "Dammit, you should have had an injection last night—woulda helped this swelling."

"I know. I just didn't think of it last night," I muttered, feeling very embarrassed by everything.

"Are you going to press charges—and before you say anything, the right answer is yes."

"The way those police acted, I don't see what good it will do."

"Well, you have to try. I'm going to give you this card. On the back is a man's name and number. Keep it on your bedstand, and if Jack comes to hurt you again, call this man. He'll make sure Jack never bothers you again."

"He won't kill him, will he?" I asked.

He smiled and said, "He'll just make him wish he was dead, and he won't bother you again. Go see the DA, Susan."

The next day, I decided that I would do just that. It was around 1978, and in Kansas at that time, it was still a man's world. As I stepped into the DA's office, a bunch of men turned to look at me. It was a fairly small town, and they knew who I was and what I ate for dinner last night. I straightened up as tall as I could and said to the DA, "I want to press charges against someone for trying to kill me." I waited a few seconds while they all looked at me, some smirking, and before I could say any more, the DA said, "What's your problem? You're still alive, aren't you?" I'll never forget that comment and the contemptuous look on his face. Clearly I wasn't worth any effort on his part. I know now there were other things I could have done, but I just tucked my tail and left. I know my face was brick red, and Jack's fingerprints on my neck were even clearer. I went home and felt sorry for myself. As far as I know, the police record there still says that I started the fight. Unbelievable! So much grief, so much anger and sadness. I felt like the real world had passed me by, and I didn't know why. From the time I was a child with parents who didn't want me to that day, I didn't seem to be able to hold onto someone who loved me. It was a pity party for me. I felt the sourness of life's broken plans, life's dashed dreams.

My kids were my love, and we were so close. I jokingly told people that we grew up together, and in a way we did. Every day I told them that I loved them, and I always made sure I told them the truth. Sam and Sally were also wise beyond their years, because I held nothing back from them.

They knew what I knew. We were a tight threesome. And, boy, did that ever pay off. Nothing could come between my two kids and me. Nothing.

It was about this point in time when I thought of a grand idea! For the kids and I were going to go on a summer vacation! We were going to have our first real vacation. I started planning everything with the kids at my side. We decided that we'd take the southern route to California and the northern route back home. We got maps (no GPS then) and started laying out our routes. Now, mind you, my car was a VW412! Some people thought I was foolish to go so far alone with two kids in a VW but I thought it was a great adventure! The kids did, too. I had enough medical supplies crammed in that car to open a small clinic – my friends thought of every possible contingency. My boss was very happy for me and granted my three week off request. Boy, with each day that passed, Dam, Sally and I got more and more excited. Sam was going to be the navigator in the passenger seat and Sally was the log keeper and was in the back of the VW – she's never let go of that.

We trekked right through the desert with no difficulty although we saw a lot of vehicles whose radiators were smoking. The sights were awesome as we toured the Hoover Dam, the Painted Desert and other famous places. We stayed in Las Vegas one night and went into the casinos to see what they were like. Really didn't excite us that much. When we got to San Diego, we stayed with some Navy friends who took us to Tijuana, Mexico. Right before we crossed the border, one of my friends jokingly asked "Does anyone have any guns?" I replied without even thinking, "yes, I have a pistol in my purse". Our friend, Joe, almost collapsed right there as he looked at me with wild eyes "OMG – we have to go back to the car and put that gun in the car! If you take that across the border, you'll be in jail in Mexico!" Needless to say, that's what we did. Boy, that was a scary moment in time. I was so thankful that Joe haphazardly asked about guns! For years after that incident, every time we talked, we always howled about the 'gun story'.

Disneyland was so magical for all three of us. What memories we had there. We stayed there a couple of days and then started our trip up the California coast to the Hearst Mansion. That mansion was mind-boggling in terms of pure wealth. I was very interested in its history and owner. Next we went to the Redwood Forest where an absolutely hilarious thing happened. Remember that my Sammy was always the prankster? Well, while walking through the forest, I couldn't keep from farting, so I did – never thinking of how the sound would echo in that huge forest. Echo it did….like you wouldn't believe. I pulled off the best, I mean THE best, performance ever as I conjured up this expression of disdain and turned to face my son among all the tourists and hissed "Sam, how could you?"

Then, with my nose in the air, I turned and pranced off in the other direction. Everyone thought Sam did it! Payback for all those pranks!

We started our trip home after that momentous event but we stopped at Salt Lake City to check out the lake and the Mormon Tabernacle Choir. Everything was great but the kids didn't like the lake. Being saltwater, it stung. So, off we went toward Colorado. We were a little nervous in the mountains because the VW acted like it was on its last leg. I remember Sammy saying, "Mom, I don't think it's going to make it up this mountain". But we climbed it slowly and steadily – in the slow lane they had for vehicles like ours. Steamboat Springs, Colorado is where I almost got arrested. It happened so innocently. I was the first car in the left lane pulled up at red light. On my left were vehicles in the left turn lane. I saw a police car just a couple of cars behind me in the right lane. I told the kids, "Oh, oh, there's the cops". For some unknown reason, when the left turn lane got their green arrow and started moving, I did, too!! What a dolt. Needless to say, the cop pulled me over. The rest was hysterical. He asked me for my driver's license which I nervously produced and then he asked me for my car registration. That I DIDN'T have! In Kansas in those days, we didn't keep our registration papers in the car. Now, being a complete nervous wreck, I took all the papers I had in my glove box and gave them to this cop. Everything was in there, including my divorce papers – everything but the registration. I looked at him and said, "Officer, really, who would want this car – it's a VW. It's not like I'm driving a BMW or something!

He looked at me – oh, he was really a hunk – and, with a little grin on one side on his mouth, said "Do you see that motel over there? If you go there right now and spend the night there, I won't give you a ticket." "Hallelujah! I'm on my way"! No jail, no ticket. Of course, that's what I did.

Our vacation was the best thing we ever did and every time we were together over the years, we look at our log and talk about this trip. By the way, Sam is still peeved about the Redwood Forest caper.

Back home, one evening, I answered the phone at home to hear Johnny's soft voice. "Chicky, how are you?"

I choked as I cried out loud, "Johnny, Johnny, are you okay?"

"Sure, Chicky, I'm fine. It's just that, well, I'm here in town, not far from your house!"

"What? How did you get here? What are you doing here? Oh, Johnny, can I see you?" My heart was racing, and I felt the tears on my cheeks as I waited to hear his answer.

"Chicky, I want to see you, too. In fact, I have this idea.

If you can arrange a sitter for the kids, let's go away together for the weekend. I know it's wrong, but it's also right. We have always loved each other and never had even a day together. I can't leave my family any more than you can leave yours. Can't we have a weekend together though? If we're careful, who will it hurt? Don't we deserve even that, after all we've lived through?"

I knew it was wrong, but my heart won.

We got it all arranged. I went to meet Johnny the next weekend in Wichita, Kansas. He had reserved a suite at a very nice hotel, and we met there. I will always remember waiting for him in the lobby. When I saw him come in the door, I went weak at the knees. I ran to him and threw, myself in his arms, crying out, "Johnny, I've always loved you." He picked me up off my feet, and with his warm lips pressed to mine, he twirled me around the foyer. I can still see the guy at the desk smiling broadly as he watched us.

That weekend was the greatest time of my personal life. Johnny and I had always been soul mates, and now we were lovers, too. I had never been loved like this man loved me. He touched me so softly, caressing every part of me. We had soaks in the large tub together with candles and scents—just like the movies. No one had every treated me so grandly, and I reveled in it all. In bed, he knelt behind me and caressed my whole body from behind. I burned from his touch. "Johnny, I love you," I whispered.

"Chicky, we have always loved each other, and we always will. I love you, Chicky," he said as he softly stroked my face—just like he had years and years before.

It was the weekend of my life. We went out when we were hungry. It was a fairy-tale moment in time for us both, and we never wanted it to end. But we both knew it had to. "Chicky," Johnny sighed, "it is so hard to say goodbye. We're going to be together—I know it, just not right now."

God, I thought, *Johnny is so cool—his touch, his voice, his kiss—oh, how I long to be with him when I go to sleep at night, when I wake up in the morning. I never thought I'd feel this way.* We were just dance partners, but over the years I'd learned one thing: he was the best. I wished I'd realized that years ago.

We danced softly—no rock and roll. "A Man Loves a Woman" played, and as the song played on, we grew closer and closer. Our bodies moved as one, and I snuggled my face into his chest, loving his smell and the ruggedness of his body and his litheness, like that of a cougar.

Then, in a nanosecond it seemed, the music was over. "Chicky, we have to get going so we make it to the airport on time." I heard the catch in his voice, and it brought tears to my eyes. *I know now that it's Johnny I have always loved, and he loves me. But we can't be together. Oh God, how cruel! It never works out for me—never.*

We left the gorgeous hotel room that I would remember forever, but oddly never with a sense of guilt. We were pretty quiet as we rode in the taxi to the airport, but we held onto each other all the way. We were at the airport in what seemed like seconds, and I wanted nothing more than to stay with this man forever. But I knew I couldn't. Sally and Sam were waiting for me.

It was time for us to say our goodbye, but Johnny held me tight, his fingers stroking my face like he always did, as he tilted his head down to mine. With the lightest but sweetest voice, he whispered, "Not yet, Chicky, but soon." He turned and walked away.

"Bye, Johnny." I felt my lips moving but no sound came out as I slowly walked into my Jetway. "Johnny," I sobbed, but he couldn't see me or hear me anymore as people pushed and shoved around me. I didn't care if I was trampled to death—right then, right there. But life went on, and I wasn't done yet.

CHAPTER 6

LOOK AT ME!

Just like this is a new chapter in my book, my life began a new chapter. I entered the world of health care management. I was so excited to be promoted, get more money, and realize that someone valued what I did. My work hours changed, too, so I could be more available for my kids. But let me tell you now, there is a price for all this, and it is you! You now belong to the organization. When you're needed, you have to be there.

I also continued to do clinical work so I wouldn't lose my skills and because I loved it. I worked in the ED when they were short, and I worked as a house supervisor frequently. It was a fast-paced job with something new practically every minute—like the day a psych patient jumped out a tenth- floor window and landed in a construction mud pit.

I was first on the scene and had to dig the mud from her mouth so I could do mouth-to-mouth. Long story short, she broke everything from her waist up, but it took her about six hours to die. Then we had law enforcement all over the place, and even the FBI. It was an awful thing, because this patient was only in her thirties, and it shouldn't have happened, but it did. Her family wanted to sue, and we ended up settling out of court. This was mainly because we didn't have bars on the windows, and the patients could open them.

One funny piece to all this was when the FBI wanted to fingerprint the windowsill and found out there were no fingerprints. That's because the nuns in housekeeping had already cleaned the windowsill. You should have seen the agent's face. Well, our hospital was very clean.

Here came the eighties with the entrance of HMOs and other health care experiments. Most clinical people hated all of it, because it did no good for the patients. You couldn't argue that our health care was too expensive, and we abused the system from time to time—like admitting someone's grandmother to the hospital so the family could take a vacation and then bill Medicare for it. Those things were wrong, but the solutions in the eighties and nineties were wrong, too.

Watching the paradox of the changing world of health care during those years was as hard as anything we'd ever experienced. Nonclinical people were making decisions about patients' health care. How could that work? It was the beginning of the transformation that didn't fully take root until Obamacare decades later. Watching this as a nurse manager inspired me to write my one and only parody:

Is It a Revolution or a Nightmare?
A parody that illustrates a nurse manger's response to managed care
Once upon a midnight dreary, while I pondered weak and weary,
Over many a quaint, boring volume of JCAHO regulations,
While I nodded, nearly napping, suddenly there came a tapping,
As of someone gently rapping, rapping at my office door.
"Tis someone to complain again," I muttered, "Tapping at my office door, and nothing more."

Open wide I flung the door, when with great flutter
In stepped a stately raven from days of yore. Without a second, he perched above my office door,
Perched and sat, and nothing more.

My eyes I rubbed, hoping I would wake to see a dream and not this scary sight,
When suddenly this grim bird heralded my first visitor of this long night!
There, like he was made of mist and smoke, appeared a staff MD
With his fists clenched and his face tight.

"I did that training you wanted for your staff,
　　But your nurses still aren't doing it right!"

Before I could blink, he was gone, and in his
　　place stood our CEO,
Angrily banging his fist on my books.
"I can't believe it, but you let those FTEs go
　　up *again*,"
He screeched with threatening looks!

With great anxiety, I closed my eyes, and
　　when I opened them again,
I saw my only full-time night RN in a terrible
　　fit.
Tears ran down her face as she sadly said,
　　"You promised me more days off months
　　ago!
I can't do this anymore. It's just too hard! I
　　quit!"

I stood stunned as another visitor, the
　　daughter of a patient,
Darted through the door with a disgusted
　　and angry glare!
"Dad had no bath all week! His hair's dirty,
　　his room's a mess, and his teeth are lost.
You call this a hospital? Don't tell me this is
　　care!"

Alone at last, and to still the beating of my
　　heart, I sunk down in my chair.
Once again, that ghostly fowl perched itself
　　above my office door.

I searched that sleek bird's ancient, yellow
    eyes
And cried out, "When will this be over?
    When will it be like it was before?"

With its black plumes fluttering, its fiery eyes
    glaring,
The demon bird croaked just one word—

"Nevermore!"

Believe me, I got a lot of flack for this when it was published. I kept asking everyone, "Do you know what a parody is? It's only a parody!" I didn't write anything else— at least for several years.

Being in the management world opened another chapter of my education—the world of double standards. In health care, that often meant docs. Talk about special treatment, even if the guy's a drunk, like the one who hurt my back when I was a new nurse. The system protected these people because "society needs them." I guess society didn't care about me; it sure didn't feel like it most of my life.

There were many others like him. They did a variety of things for which they weren't punished or, in some cases, even challenged. One of our cardiologists developed dementia and was so bad that he didn't know what floor he was on when he was in the hospital. Nonetheless, no one reported all this. All of us checked and corrected his orders until finally his family got him someplace safe where he could be cared for. Point is, we didn't take care of the problem. I saw that over and over.

And, of course, the extramarital affairs of these doctors were legend. The nurses were just as bad; most of them would screw any doctor just to say they did. They left their families for one affair after another. I believe that this was a symptom of the angst we as nurses and doctors experienced in our work day in and day out.

Flashback to Charles. I will never be able to explain how I felt about Charles. I loved him in a different way than I loved Johnny, but love them both, I did. Even though Charles was gay and we never even had an affair, it was okay. I loved him anyway. Neither of us was married at the time, and he never was. For the first couple of years of our relationship, I thought I could help him be "normal," but that wasn't to be. Still, we had the greatest relationship, and we loved each other in a platonic way.

We went everywhere together. He bought me beautiful things, some of which I still have. I think I got my sense of class from him. He was very distinguished looking and acting. He had black hair and hazel eyes and was about four inches taller than me. We danced, we entertained, we traveled, we did everything but live together or have a sexual relationship. I wanted to be with him day and night, but I was okay with what I had. I got to be with him a lot, and that was better than if I'd walked away. Charles and I were together for nine or ten years.

On a sadder note, one dark day after Charles's mother had died and he felt he could be who he was publicly, he told me what I didn't want to hear. "Sis, (he always called me Sis—kind of like Johnny calling me Chicky), I have to do something different. I have to be who I am, and I'm going to have to relocate to do it. I want you to stay here— you have your kids. You need to finish raising them, and I need to do this. You and I both know that we will always love each other. Remember our special saying: *jamais je ne t'oublierai, toujours je t'aimerai par toute l'eternite,*" he said softly, ending that difficult conversation with our favorite French phrase. Roughly translated, it means "I will never forget you, and I will love you forever through all eternity." And he was gone.

We talked frequently, but I missed him so much. It wasn't long after that that he got AIDS and died, as I described earlier. Life rolled on, though, and a few months after Charles' death, Jerry Masters, a guy at work asked me for a date. I had known him for years—in fact, he was married to one of my nursing school friends, but they were divorced. "Susan, he said, "we go to our kids' games all the time; we might as well go to them together and be a little company to each other."

So, Jerry and I began to date. It wasn't love at first sight by any means, at least for me. He was nice enough and had very gentle brown eyes. He just wasn't my type. I liked the Irish look—from my dad, I guess.

Before long, we were dating and not just going together to our kids' games. We worked together, too. He managed pediatrics and I managed a medical-surgical unit. We seldom saw each other during the day, but we were beginning to be together a lot in the evenings. The kids seemed to think it was all very natural.

Of course, it couldn't just go along like that. Jerry really wanted to be with me, was very kind-hearted, and seemed to care for me. One day he said, "Susan, I love you, and you say you love me, so what's the problem? Why can't we talk about it to others and especially the kids? What do you want from this? It just can't keep going on the way it is. You know that, right?"

I was afraid of a commitment after my first marriage, but I knew Jerry was a good man, and I liked being with him. Was I crazy in love with him? No. No bells were ringing, no stars in my eyes. I remembered something my mother told me once, and how awful I thought her comment was. "Susan, you don't marry someone you love; you marry someone who loves you, and the rest follows!"

I thought that was the most heartless thing I'd ever heard. "Mom, for heaven's sakes! Just because you're unhappy doesn't mean everyone else thinks they're doomed to a life of misery," I would tell her. "Most of us do love our mates, or at least we did at one time." And there I was with Jerry, feeling pretty much like my mother was right there telling me, "I told you so!"

After a few months of dating, Jerry and I got married on December 31, 1977. Someone told us that if we got married before the New Year started, we'd save a lot on taxes. Well, married we were, but it saved nothing on our taxes. Life is one lesson after another.

Jerry and I weren't married a week when he said, "Susan, if you could be anyone in the world or do anything in the world, what would it be?"

Now, that's a heavy question that should take a person some time to answer. Not me, no—I spit out the answer in seconds. "I'd like to be a high school English teacher." We were discussing that idea and what it would take for me to be able to do that when Jerry pounded the table where we were sitting and said, "Let's make it happen,"

He grinned from ear to ear, and he did it. He got a second mortgage on his home to finance my college courses. Is that not the sweetest thing anyone could do for someone else? I was stunned by his care and consideration for me.

So, off to school I went, having resigned from my position at the hospital so I could be a full-time student. I had a double major: English and education. Those were the days! I thoroughly enjoyed myself as I studied English literature, American literature, and writing. It was so enjoyable that I hated to see it end. My GPA was great—somewhere around 3.9. I also had to take the entrance exam for teaching in Kansas and thought it would be where the rubber met the road. But I did okay!

My teaching career was launched in a small rural high school where I was hired to teach College Prep English, Creative Writing, and Practical English. I had five classes a day with three different courses. As every teacher knows, a good part of my day was spent babysitting some of the students. Still, I loved it—even more than nursing. There wasn't a day that I didn't feel like I made a difference in a young person's life and future. I often jokingly said that I didn't teach English, I taught Life.

I taught for three and a half years at that little school and won the Teacher of the Year Award three years in a row. The award was given by the student body to the teacher they deemed appropriate. That award meant a great deal to me then and still does today.

Then there was a catastrophic event. One of the juniors had a car accident right in front of the school. We actually heard it. Of course, lots of the teachers and students ran out to see what happened, including me, to find that it was a single-vehicle accident and that the driver was one of our own—one of the kids recognized the car. I ran to the car, and as I approached it, I heard that distinctive sound (if you're in the medical field, you recognize it immediately) of fluid gurgling in an airway. This is incompatible with life.

The student was unconscious and was drowning in his own saliva. To make matters worse, his head was turned in an abnormal position. It looked like his legs were both broken as well. I knew my first task was to open his airway without hurting his spine. I proceeded to do that through the window that was broken out and managed to position myself so that I could open his airway and protect his spine in the process. I knew when I had it pretty good, because the gurgling sound went away for the most part.

Blood was everywhere, and I, of course, was wearing a white blouse. As I held his airway open, waiting for the EMTs to get there, my principal came running over to me to ask me if he could do anything. My answer was pretty grim, "Frank, get all the students out of here. I smell gas.

This car could blow. Get them and everyone else out of here, Frank. You, too."

"What about you, Susan?"

"Frank, if I let go of his head, he will die. Period. He will die. I can't do that, so I have to take my chance. Now go and see that everyone else is okay." As Frank walked away and began shepherding everyone away, I felt very alone, scared, and hopeful that the EMTs would get there soon. I couldn't bring myself to walk away from that young man. I had to keep him breathing.

It seemed like forever, but finally I heard the sirens and saw the fire department trucks and the EMTs in their ambulance round the corner. What a great sight that was to me! Rescue was coming right toward me. It was old home week at first as the responders saw me and I saw them. As an ER nurse, I knew these guys. One of them took over for me with the boy's airway, and I was greatly relieved that he did. My arm muscles were really sore, too.

The boy lived and returned to school several months later. The whole schools saw me as the hero in that event, but as all health care workers know, being a hero only means you did your job. So teaching was a great career that included many stories like the ones above, stories that reinforce how powerful and rewarding teaching can be. I don't know how it is now, but teachers in Kansas didn't make very much money.

Marriage to Jerry was like moving from the Earth to Mars. One day there was me, Sally, and Sam, and the next day there was Jerry, me, Sally, Buck, Bradley, Sam, Mason, and Karly. It felt like the Brady Bunch. We were always out of hot water, clean towels, and milk. Cooking breakfast reminded me of the air force mess hall, but I loved it. I was enjoying the beauty of being with a man who loved me. Jerry loved loving me, if you understand what I mean. Jack never took the time.

My mother, who was highly uncomfortable with anything that even came close to being about sex, didn't tell me the things most mothers help their daughters be prepared for. And since I had very few to no friends and didn't date, I couldn't learn from those experiences either.

So picture me, a woman in her late thirties with two kids, learning about lovemaking. What's the chance of that happening unless you were in a convent? So Mom was right: marry someone who loves you, and everything will fall in place. Jerry clearly loved me, so I began to think of him in a different way. And finally I knew that I loved him, too.

We had a lot of challenges, mostly related to money, with all the kids we had. But we made do, and life was grand. We also had a lot of arguments, especially in the beginning. But after two or three years, we were past all that as well.

We lived on a large estate, complete with its own manmade pond, a bridge, and trickling waters. Jerry stocked the pond, and he allowed all the neighborhood kids to fish there. In fact, that's why he had it in the first place. The house was a huge two-story Colonial-era home, so there was room for all of us, but things were tight. I think the kids had a hard time adjusting, too.

Jerry and I worked together at the hospital, and we worked together at home. He was a hard worker, and he expected no less from all of us. It seemed like we were always in the middle of a building or landscaping project.

Sometimes we resented that and bemoaned our fate to him. "Do we have to do this again? Why don't we just buy something like everyone else does," we whined.

"Keep working. We're burning daylight" was his usual reply.

What we created became a legacy, and we didn't even know it. Everyone in our area called our place Master's Pond, but we didn't know that for years. People asked us if they could be married there, and we always said yes. Jerry's mother always warned him that somebody was going to get hurt there, especially because of the pond, and we'd be sued. Jerry never slowed down in his passion to serve children, no matter what anyone said.

So every year, Master's Pond saw a new generation of kids who learned to fish there. One year, as we dredged the pond—a disgusting job because of the god-awful stench that emanated from it—but we did it anyway. That year, a special treat awaited me. I was sweating like I don't know what when I felt something tickle my shoulder. I looked down out of the side of my glasses and clearly saw a gigantic, black, hairy tarantula sitting there on my shoulder. It was tantamount to a nightmare turned real.

Instinctively, I swatted it off my shoulder and started letting everyone in hearing range know how I felt about being attacked by that creature. Of course, I got no sympathy from the group. Then there was the day I nailed my foot to a two-by-four with a sixteen-penny nail. In the early days with Jerry, I couldn't tell you what a sixteen-penny nail was, and a two-by-four was a piece of medical gauze to me. By the end of our building /renovating time together, I was a master apprentice. No kidding.

I'm still pretty knowledgeable about renovations/ construction. I actually came to enjoy the work and loved being able to see what I accomplished every day with my own two hands. It was very rewarding, especially when I was finally able to move into the new bedroom/bathroom we built together. Sweet!

One day, in the middle of all this fun, a giant, gorgeous dog entered our lives. He was supposed to be a Russian wolf hound, and he was to be my dog. Jerry knew I always wanted a dog like that, partly for security reasons. One day, he flew in the door after work and told me he found a Russian wolf hound for me. "Are you sure?" I asked. "There are so few of them in this part of the country."

"Yes," he said, "he is a Russian wolf hound. This military couple has him, and they've been given orders to a place where they can't take dogs. They don't even want any money, just a good home for him."

I was elated—finally I'd have the dog I'd always wanted. We went out to see the dog, and when I was led up to the cage where he stayed when everyone was gone, I couldn't believe my eyes. Before me was the most beautiful animal I had ever seen, but he was not a Russian wolf hound. He was an Afghan hound. His stage name was Magic, because he was solid black, but when he pranced and raised those front legs high, the hair parted and silver sparkled from beneath the black hair. Everywhere we went, people thought he was a bear. When he stood on his hind feet, his head was above mine. He was magnificent. I ended up naming him Yuri, after Yuri Zhivago—well, he was supposed to be a Russian wolf hound, so I gave him a Russian name.

So my saga at Master's Pond continued. It was an idyllic time in one way and a sweathouse in another. My husband loved me—that was the idyllic part and an experience I had never really had. He taught me how a man should make love to a woman—ah, that was definitely the best I've ever felt.

At the same time, though, he was a workaholic, and all of us worked along with him. Those who knew him called him Johnny Appleseed because he loved to plant things and grow them. He was, indeed, a would-be farmer. So we planted everything there is to plant. But he was most famous for the pond. He also used railroad ties as the fence line of the property—all five acres. At the juncture of the ties, he planted red climbing roses—his favorite. That meant five acres of roses for me to tend. The grass was like velvet, and we mowed something almost every day.

At Christmastime, we strung lights on the beautiful big fir trees on our property, and we did it all in a row, each of us carrying our section of the lights. When we were done, we would stand there in the dark and wait for Jerry to throw the switch. It was always a time of oohs and aaahs. "Okay, kids, it's time for us to go into the house and have hot chocolate," I'd call to the kids as we started to the house. They loved the part where we had hot chocolate and buttered toast. So did I! I made piles of toast, and everyone grabbed some and started dipping it in their hot chocolate. I can smell it right now! We all loved the warmness in our bellies and the steam on our glasses—a memory forever.

Jerry was a pediatric RN, as I mentioned before and was loved by everyone who knew him. His kindness and love for children was legendary in our community, and the pond made it even better. We cleaned the pond out every year and restocked it with fish for the kids. Some caught their very first fish at that pond, and that made Jerry very happy. We had six children altogether plus Yuri, who became like another child. Jerry loved that dog, and he loved Jerry—the guy who had never had a dog.

Yuri was supposed to be mine, but clearly that was not the case. Yuri and Jerry took an obedience course, and Yuri got the dunce award. People sometimes say that Afghan hounds are stupid. They are not. They simply don't care what you want—much like cats. Yuri loved his life at Master's Pond. We all did.

One day, a couple came to our front door and introduced themselves. They were the parents whose eleven-year old girl had just died from cancer on Jerry floor at the hospital. They wanted to give Jerry a gift. "You were so wonderful with Molly," the mother said softly. "We want you to have this tree to plant in her memory. We know you are good with plants." They smiled.

This was a gift Jerry couldn't turn down. This was something he could do for that family and for that child. So he took the tree from them, and we told them goodbye. As I looked at the tree, I saw that its leaves were fan-shaped, and I realized it was a gingko. Jerry planted it and nurtured it, and it grew and grew.

Then, one spring, Jerry suffered a devastating myocardial infarction (a heart attack) that blew out his left ventricle and left him with a cardiac ejection fraction of 11 percent—incompatible with life, according to most docs. So he ended up being diagnosed with end-stage heart disease when he was forty- four. Our life at Master's Pond was over. Everything was sold at a sheriff's sale, and we moved to a small house that I could manage on my own.

Whatever heart Jerry had left was broken by the loss of the place he loved so much, Master's Pond. It was gone from our daily lives but never from our hearts. Jerry lived, if you could call it that, for another eleven years, even though his prognosis had been six months. That prognosis was horrible in and of itself. As we got closer to the six months, we thought every day would be his last. When it came and passed, it was a surreal feeling. We didn't know what to think of this gift of life beyond what we were told. The human spirit is incredible.

During that six months and while we waited for Jerry's 'last day', he looked over at me one morning while we were still at the breakfast table and said, "I wish I could make one last trip to see all the places I've never seen and would like to see". I was kind of stunned because I didn't know there were places he wanted to see. "Geez, hon", I said, "you've never mentioned this before". "I know" he answered, looking at me with his big puppy dog, brown eyes. I thought there'd be a time later, when we retired ...". "Oh, that makes sense. So where would you like to go?

"Well, I've always wanted to see Montana, Wyoming, Oregon and even California", he said with a deep sigh.

I sat there with him thinking and finally said, "I think we should do it!" We've got a decent RV and a fairly new pickup that could pull it just fine. Wouldn't need hotels so that would save us some dollar", I quipped.

Jerry looked over at me with a sad smile, "it would be hard on you because I wouldn't be able to drive much".

"Jerry, I am good with this. You start looking at the places you want to see and I'll put in for three weeks of vacation, starting the first of June, okay?" As I looked at Jerry, I saw his famous ear-to-ear grin light up his face. Yep, his wheels were turning already – no pun intended!

We started getting all the supplies we needed ready for this huge trip after we talked to Jerry's docs and got their permission and assistance. We would need to carry a large oxygen cylinder plus various medications, including intravenous (IV) morphine. Jerry worked on our routes and places he wanted to see. We started stocking the RV with food and other supplies, getting excited as we did. I was happy to see Jerry excited about something positive. I probably didn't mention it but I was a little nervous – I drove standard shift cars before but this pickup was huge and the stick was on the floor and was as big as me! Plus I had never pulled anything. In fact, I was horrible at backing up with the riding lawnmower and its attachments!

Nonetheless, on a bright June morning, off we went one our road trip. Everything went smoothly on the open highways and flat roads we had in Kansas. We stayed at various RV parks along the way. Then we got to Colorado and started up into the mountains. Here is where I met my first challenge. Stopping at a stop sign on a hill caused me to almost burn up the clutch, trying to get up that hill from a stop. But, we made it. Jerry only swore a couple of times.

Worse though, we hadn't counted on what the higher elevations would do to Jerry's oxygen saturation and it wasn't good! I noticed that he was getting confused in things he said and finally realized what was happening, so I pulled over at a rest stop to adjust his oxygen level and make sure all the connections were good. Jerry went into the bathroom while I did that. I was just about through doing all that when I heard this pounding – it was coming from the bathroom! I went over and opened the door and there stood Jerry with this 'I don't know where I am' look on his face. I realized that the pounding I heard was Jerry trying to find the door from the inside of the BR. I was momentarily thrown completely off kilter.

The next morning the sun rose beautifully as we sat at our RV table and enjoyed our own eggs and bacon. Things were good again so we started off on our trip after breakfast. Jerry loved the Dakotas and wanted to start life all over in Montana! He loved the wide open spaces. Then we headed toward Washington. Somewhere on a major highway east of Seattle, disaster struck again – this time in the form of another heart attack. Suddenly Jerry clutched his chest, crying out in pain, "Oh, no", he said, "I think I'm having another heart attack." His doctors had warned us that this would probably happen after the devastating heart attack he had has, due to the extensive damage his heart had sustained.

I pulled over as soon as I could and got my IV supplies out from the back seat as well as the morphine and went over to Jerry to assess his status. I checked his blood pressure, pulse, heart sounds and skin color. His skin was cyanotic (bluish) and clammy and his pain level as a 'ten' on the pain scale that all health care practitioners used to evaluate pain. It goes from 'one' to 'ten' with 'ten' being the worst pain. My assessment led me to believe that Jerry was suffering from another heart attack and that I needed to inject some morphine so I got the syringe ready and prepared his arm for an injection. As I was injecting a morphine cartridge, all of a sudden, a state trooper pulled up behind us. When he looked at us through the driver's window, I saw his eyes widen when he saw that I was injecting something into this man's arm.

I quickly addressed the situation, "Officer, I'm an R.N. and this is my husband. He is having a heart attack and I'm administering morphine IV for the pain. I have a prescription for the morphine".

"Ma'am, I'll get your husband to the nearest hospital in a hurry – just follow me".

"Officer, you don't understand. My husband doesn't want medical care because he's dying and nothing can be done to reverse that. I have all the paperwork, signed by his physician in Kansas where we live, to confirm what I'm telling you. We are on this trip so he can see the places he wanted to see before he died. We appreciate your offer to help very much but just want to go on with our trip when he feels better.

That officer, a very young guy, was great! He did review my paperwork, made a call on his radio and then told us that he would stay with us until we were ready to get back on the road unless he got called to respond to another matter. We told him 'goodbye' when we pulled out.

We drove all over the State of Washington, saw many beautiful panoramas of the state and of Whidbey Island off the coast of Washington. It was quite picturesque. We drove over the one bridge that went into Whidbey Island that crossed Deception Pass. Usually, it was covered in fog. We had a peaceful few days. It was a healing time.

The coastline of Washington and Oregon was simply awesome, especially to people who lived in Kansas!

As we drove along down the Oregon coastal highway, one beautiful morning, suddenly our pull-along RV unhitched itself and we were in trouble! I hit the brakes – not much help with this fully loaded RV on the other end of our pickup. I really didn't fully understand what this meant at the time but I could see Jerry knew it was bad and that was unnerving. Thank God, we came to a stop several yards before the cliffs! Turns out that what saved us was that the road had been blacktopped and the hitch on the RV dug into the fresh asphalt and that slowed us down.

We got out to survey the damage and talked with all the folks who saw it happen. "Boy", I said – "I'm glad we didn't lose the pickup. Some of our major supplies are in the back of the pickup plus we'd have nothing to drive. Jerry looked at me with this incredulous look as he said, "Susan, if the RV went over, the pickup would have followed. See those chains? We would have lost everything, up to and possibly including us! That's when I got sick to my stomach.

Our trip was terrifying, wonderful, peaceful and exhausting, all at the same time. The last escapade we had on our trip was a little on the funny side. Jerry wanted something to eat from McDonald's. We were on the last leg of our trip. I spotted the Golden Arch as we neared some town and pulled off to get Jerry what he wanted. I never once thought about the height of the RV!! Once I pulled in and rounded the curve, I immediately saw that we couldn't possibly fit. Oh, I thought, what do I do now?

Jerry said, "you'll have to back up". Well, that comment struck terror in my heart – me – backup this rig?? OMG! I got out of the truck and walked toward the back of the RV so I could see how to back up. Of course, by now, there were a gazillion other cars lined up behind me. I looked at all those people and just started yelling, "if you want to keep your car like it is, you better get out of the way because I have to back this thing up in order to get it out of here!" Nobody gave me any trouble and everyone got out of the way. I was hoping someone would offer to back it up for me but no such luck.

I jumped back into the truck and put it in reverse and slowly backed up. When I went over the curb, that RV swayed like you wouldn't believe. I was so scared that we were going to flip over, I was praying for all I was worth. After what seemed like forever, we were out! I pulled into a straightaway and shut her down. I was sweating. Jerry told me that I was one brave soul and I loved him for that.

So, I walked inside and got Jerry what he wanted and took it out to him. We savored that food! Some of the people who backed out of the way, came over to tell us how hard that would have been for them to do.

We ended our infamous trip a few days after that incident. Even though it was a trip filled with misadventures, I never regretted taking Jerry to see everything he wanted to see.

A corollary to my husband's illness was that I had to go back to work as a nurse so I could make as much money as I could. I was very sad to leave my students, but I had no choice. So back to the hospital I went. It was another crushing blow for Jerry and me, but as I told him, "I have my memories, memories that I will cherish forever."

In the midst of all this, my parents decided to move from Ohio to Kansas. I was shell-shocked. I was speechless. I wondered, How is this going to work? Well, when they got there and settled in, I held a conference with them. It wasn't really a family conference, because we were never family. I told them that what they did to me as a child was mind- boggling and that I would never forget it. "But," I added, "I am going to forgive it. You are my parents, and I will respect that."

Without even a tear, I told my mother that I would never understand why she didn't come to check on me when she got home from wherever she was every night. I said, "When I get home from work at night, the first place I go to see that my kids are safe and asleep in their beds. Isn't that what every mother does? But you never did that for me. You never, not once, came to see where I was."

I looked at them both, thinking I would hear some rationale, but they just looked at me. And so began another chapter in my life: taking care of Jerry and taking care of my parents. Go figure! We found a house for them close to where we now lived so we wouldn't have to drive across town to get there when they needed us. After they were all established and found a church for Mom, life went on like it was. Mom and Dad didn't need much then, and we generally went to dinner together on Sunday.

Actually a great gift came from my parents' move to Kansas to be with me. This is why we should always remember that when something bad happens, it may be setting the stage for something great to happen later. My mother was the first of my parents to get sick and die. She had lung cancer. But then my father began to talk about his life before Mom. He told me he was married to another woman before Mom and had two sons. "Dad," I screeched, "you're kidding, right? I spent my whole life trying to be a son for you—learned all about cars and motors, learned to change the oil, the tires, the sparkplugs. You're joking, aren't you?"

"No, Susan, I'm not. One of the boys was named for me, and I want to know what happened to them. I haven't seen or heard from them since I left them when they were one and two years old. I know you're good on the computer, and I thought you could find them for me."

I was so stunned, I could hardly talk. I went to my computer and did a search for Stephen Allen Hemblein Jr. There was one hit, and it was him—Dad's second son. Somehow I managed to get the phone number and called. A woman answered who I later learned was Stephen's wife, Helen. "Are you selling something," she asked.

"Well, I guess in a way I am. I think I'm related to your husband. May I speak to him?"

I heard some background noise, and the line went dead. I said, "Dad, I don't think they want to talk to you." Dad just kinda hung his head. That was the end of that, I thought.

But a couple of weeks later, I got a surprise phone call. "Susan," the man said, "my name is Stephen Allen Hemblein Jr., and I accidentally disconnected the phone when you called my home a few days ago. It took me a while to find your phone number. You know, I always thought I had a sister!" It was time for me to be stunned again. I had two half-brothers I never knew existed, and they had a sister.

Both brothers, Stephen and Joe, planned to come to Kansas to be reunited with their father, our dad. You should have seen Dad while we were waiting for them to get there. He was giddy with happiness and then rigid with fear. "Dad, why are you afraid?" I asked.

"The boys had to go to an orphanage when I left them with their mother. She couldn't feed them. They were there for years until she remarried, and then she went and got them when they were around eight and nine years old. They probably hate me for that, and they're coming here to punch me good!"

"Dad, I don't think they're traveling all this way just to punch you. Why did you leave them anyway, and why didn't you ever talk to them all these years?"

"Your mom didn't want me to ever mention them to anyone. She didn't allow me to see them or talk to them. The reason I left is that one night my wife was late coming home from work, and I was taking care of the two babies and looking out the upstairs window when I saw a car pull up. And under the streetlight, I saw her get out of that car, and there were three guys in it. So I got my stuff, and as she came up the stairs to our apartment, I was going down them. I never said one word and never looked back."

"My God, Dad, you didn't even know she did anything with those guys. Didn't you ask?"

"Nope, didn't need to—she was with them."

"Geez, Dad, I can't believe it. And all these years you haven't talked to them or seen them at all?"

"No, especially after Mom and I were married."

I was flabbergasted as I looked at Dad and said, "This is the most unbelievable story I've ever heard. You just walked away from her and your own two sons. Wow, no wonder you're worried about how they're going to be when they get here."

The boys flew to Kansas, rented a big Cadillac, and drove out to my place, where Dad and I were waiting. It was a little nerve-wracking, but as soon as Stephen and Joe walked in, it was clear they were great guys and wanted only to meet their dad. Dad, well, he became someone I'd never seen before. Tears rolled down his wrinkled cheeks, and all he said was "My two boys, my two boys." Stephen was quite a bit taller than Dad at six two, he looked like Dad and even used his hands like Dad did. It was uncanny. Joe was more like his mother, with blond hair and blue eyes but built like Dad. We had a great few days together before Stephen and Joe had to go home.

I think all of us had a heightened sense of belonging, of connection, that we didn't have before. We kept in contact after they got home, so Dad talked to his boys at least once a week. What a story—the kind you see in the movies or on TV. It was surreal at times as I tried to understand it all. Dad, too, was troubled by all of it. Most of all, I think, he was finally grappling with the fact that he up and walked out on those two boys, causing them to go to an orphanage for years, and they had come to see him with nothing but a desire to meet their biological father and to tell him all was well. In his world, it was an eye for an eye, so their forgiveness and love overwhelmed him.

Back to my everyday world. I was working on my master's degree and working full time as faculty in a baccalaureate nursing program, all of which required me to drive almost nine hundred miles a week from Centerville to Wichita and to Topeka. I did this for five years, getting my master's in 1999. But the worst part of it all was taking care of Jerry and watching him deteriorate every day. His pain was very difficult for both of us to deal with. It was unrelenting, and his doctors were anything but helpful.

They were concerned about their Drug Enforcement Administration license more than they were concerned about him. It was a battle we fought for years and lost on a regular basis.

Finally, in 1997, we lost the whole war when, as a patient in the very hospital where we had both trained and worked, Jerry shot and killed himself. There is no way to describe the days that followed and the shock that went through our world and the community as well. I knew why he did it and even understood it, although I could never and would never understand where he found the courage to pick up that gun, aim at his chest, and pull the trigger. I know that I couldn't do it. I just don't have whatever it takes to do it. But then, I don't live with intractable pain day in and day out like he did.

After Jerry's death, many people told me how much he meant to them for one reason or another. I wrote a tribute to him for the whole community, and I think it helped us all heal.

A Tribute to a Pediatric Nurse

On April 12, 1997, Jerry Masters died after a lengthy and difficult illness. That's the part he wouldn't want you to remember. All of us who knew Jerry, both personally and professionally, knew that children were his passion... and that's the part he would want you to remember. His work, as a pediatric RN over the span of twenty years was his mission in his life. He loved the innocence of children, the hope of children, the laughter of children, the trust of children.

It was his quiet strength, his soft, warm brown eyes and quiet voice that brought children to him like a magnet. His work with children carried over into his personal life not only in raising his own four children as well as being a stepfather to my two children, but also in the things he did at Master's Pond on Coolidge Street in Centerville, Kansas. That was a sacred place where all children could go and be safe as they fished, some for the first time, in the little pond Jerry so carefully tended and stocked for them. No matter how many times some of the children left their trash behind or broke down some of his prized roses, he never wavered in his intent that any child would be welcome at Master's Pond. I can still see a very small little boy who rang our doorbell one morning to tell us with great excitement that he had just caught his first fish (it was almost as long as he was tall!) and he asked Jerry if he could keep this fish. Jerry kneeled down to talk with him and tell him that fish was his because he caught it. How proud and thrilled that little boy was! I can't help but wonder where that little boy is because I know he remembers that day. So many people over all the years remember the pond and the fish they caught there and the man who made it all possible. Jerry loved this pond for what it represented to him as a man and as a pediatric nurse. Before he died, he told me several times how much he wanted me to write about "Master's Pond" and what it meant to him. Someday, when I have the strength, I will do that.

The pond wasn't all people remember about Jerry. I think of the many times people stopped us to say, "Jerry, you probably don't remember, but you took care of my little girl or my little boy, and we cannot thank you enough for everything you did to help us." Even parents whose child died would say much the same thing. I remember on one occasion how sad Jerry was because a particular little girl on his unit was dying with cancer. After the girl died, her parents came to Jerry and said that they wanted to give him a gift to show their appreciation for all he had done. Jerry, of course, kindly refused any gift. The parents, knowing that Jerry was affectionately known as Johnny Appleseed, persisted in their desire and suggested that he at least allow them to give him a tree that he would plant at his home in their daughter's honor. Jerry accepted that idea, and the parents brought him the tree. It was a ginkgo, and I remember how strange it looked to me with its fan- shaped leaves, because I had never seen one before. Jerry tended and nurtured that tree as it began to grow, and he was happy for that.

Jerry graduated from St. Teresa's Hospital School of Nursing about 1965 as a diploma nurse, as did I. He is fondly remembered by the many nurses and staff who worked with him over the years in Maternal Child Health at St. Teresa's Hospital in Centerville. I think it would be a fair statement to say that his nurses and staff regarded him as the fairest and kindest "boss" they ever had. I think that because they said it all the time while he was alive and certainly after his death. Nurses and physicians alike admired his skills with small children. His sensitivity to children and their needs was fused into his very being. It was his art! Without a doubt, his family will always remember the insight, tenderness, and sensitivity with which he loved us as well.

Remember the ginkgo tree: Since I knew very little about this tree, I researched it on the Internet. Apparently, it is the longest-surviving species in the world, dating back some two hundred million years. In fact, it is considered a "living fossil." When Hiroshima was flattened by the atomic blast in 1945, the ginkgo was the only tree that sprouted new leaves from its blackened stumps the following spring. And the nuts from this amazing tree are used all over the world for a variety of medicinal purposes. How fitting that such a strong and enduring tree was planted in the memory of a young girl, who will live forever in that tree, planted not at the home where we no longer live, but at the grave of the pediatric nurse who worked tirelessly and lovingly for that child and all children.

Part of my master's research was about chronic pain and its devastating toll on people and families. I actually became an expert in pain management, did lectures here and there, and advised people on what they should do to handle their individual issue with pain. I was also working part time in a home health agency, and there I called upon a woman who lived alone in a small community in north-central Kansas. She was dying with renal cancer.

When I got to her home, I found her lying on her couch in her living room. She was a pleasant woman, groomed and dressed and clearly in pain. When I examined her, I was able to palpate her kidney which was not a normal finding. She was emaciated and winced at a slight touch of my hand. I asked her what she had for pain, and she said, "Tylenol— that's all my doctor wants me to take."

I contained my anger as I went to my car and called her primary care physician, whom I knew well. I told him that his patient was dying and in great pain and that perhaps he had forgotten to order pain medication for her. "No," he said. "I didn't forget. I don't think narcotics would be good for her. She's old, and she lives alone."

I carefully chose my words. "Doctor, you either give me a prescription for morphine for her right now, or I will advise her family to find another doctor. And I will call the Kansas Board of Medicine today to report you for patient abuse." He quickly capitulated, and I got my patient relief from her pain. I lined up volunteers to stay with her so she wouldn't fall or otherwise hurt herself. My patient rested for the first time in weeks. She died that week, and she died without pain.

About six months after Jerry's death, my mother died from lung cancer. She died at home on hospice and was relatively pain-free. I felt good about that. Best of all, about a week before she died, when I was rocking her in her favorite chair, she said, "Susan, I love you." That was the first and only time I ever heard my mother say she loved me. It healed a part of me.

My father, who had always loved her dearly despite his behavior, grieved for her in such tender ways that my heart ached for him. I would find little notes he wrote to her that said things like, "Mary, I saw a little bird today, and I thought of you." She loved birds. The next three years became, as I look back on it, my time with my dad. We healed our relationship completely, for which I am eternally grateful. And I took him out on Sundays for a banana split—his favorite thing in the world.

Then Dad fell and broke his hip. As nurses know, a broken hip is the beginning of the end for most elderly people, and that's what it was for him. His death was particularly painful to me. I flew his body back to Ohio to be buried in Cleveland, as we did with Mom's body. Dad was buried with full military honors due to his navy service in the Pacific Theatre during World War II.

There I was, with some of the family at the graveside, waiting for everyone to get there, when up pulled this taxi. I was stunned when I saw who was getting out of the car: it was my daughter, Sally, and I barely recognized her. I had never seen her in her dress uniform, and she had so many medals, they clinked when she walked. Her sleeves were covered with stripes.

That's when I heard one of the men in the volunteer honor guard say, "Oh shit, it's a real chief!" I was so proud of her, but I knew Dad was prouder yet. We went into the vault where the service was going to be held. The whole thing was surreal. I had buried my mother there three years earlier, but we were outside at the grave for her service. There was no honor guard for her, of course. So, there we were again, my children and me, burying their grandfather, my father. A new wrinkle, though, was that we had two brothers/uncles there to bury their father, too.

My brothers and I sat in the front row, with Sam behind me. Sally wasn't seated there, because she was the lead in the military honor guard. All of us quietly watched the detail as they folded the flag of our nation in that triangular fold with great respect and precision. Then came the moment never to be forgotten as Sally, my father's granddaughter, bent toward me with the flag between her white-gloved hands. "Mrs. Masters, on the behalf of the United States of America, we thank you for the service of your father."

As she handed me the flag, I saw her chin quiver slightly, but other than that, her military bearing was awesome. Her grandfather would have been so proud of her. They'd had a special relationship that was wonderful and one that I could never have.

The family gathered at a local restaurant before we all headed our separate ways. Sam began to tease Sally. "I saw your chin quiver," he chided. "You weren't supposed to let your emotions show, Miss Navy!" Everyone laughed and hugged each other. I felt so happy to see my children had escaped the world I grew up in. I had managed, with the grace of God, to raise them well, which was a miracle, considering my childhood.

Now both my parents were dead. What a strange, lonely feeling, I thought as I peered out the window at the restaurant. Sam somehow knew where I was in my mind as he hugged me and said, "Mom, now you're the family matriarch." I didn't like the feeling.

My grief wasn't over. No, there was one more death I would experience, and oddly it hit me the hardest. Not long after Dad died, my last Afghan hound, my beloved Lara, died. Actually, I had to put her down because she was so sick. I buried her at the gravesite where all the dogs were buried, though I had to get permission from the new owners, since we no longer lived there. I felt like my heart had been wrenched from my body as I threw the first shovel of dirt on her. I had placed her in a blanket, and when I covered her beautiful face, I wanted to die with her. I cry even now when I think of that moment. She gave me so much joy when I was so alone and so desperate. And now she was gone, too.

So a major chapter in my life closed, much as my heart closed because of all the grief around me. I sat quietly alone at night, trying to deal with all the pain. Friends came and went. I was too numb to respond. Trips to the store or to church were painful, with whispers like "there's the woman whose husband shot himself in the hospital." People turned the other way when they saw me, because they didn't know what to say. I didn't know either.

Time passed, and suddenly one morning when I rose, the world was different. I knew what I needed to do. I called my brother in Ohio, Stephen, and was stunned at the words that came out of my own mouth: "Find me a job up there, because I'm done here. I never really liked this place anyway." Three days later—yes, just three—my brother and his wife, Helen, called me with news about a job at their local hospital. They wanted a master's-prepared nursing educator. Well, that matched me to a tee. I applied, and to make a long story short, I was offered the position and accepted it. One door closed and another opened.

CHAPTER 7

A NEW ADVENTURE AT AN OLD AGE

When I look back on the decision to move, I'm amazed that I had the grit to pack up everything all by myself and move halfway across the country, leaving an entire career and lifetime of friends and contacts to start over in a small town in central Ohio, where the only person I knew was Stephen. I started my new job on September 10, 2001— one day before the World Trade Center was attacked.

I had two brothers to make up for all the family that I'd lost. I really liked Stephen's wife, Helen, and I knew off the bat we were going to be like sisters. While I was interviewing for the job, she took me everywhere, and I saw so many shops I was having a difficult time even remembering one from the other. Then she took me to the local driver's license center so I could get an Ohio license. "Helen," I said, "isn't it too soon for me to do this?"

"No," she said with a smile. "You go right on in there, and they'll take care of you."

Being the compliant soul I am, in I went. When I came out, I was distraught because they had taken my Kansas license. "Helen, what am I going to do when I go home now?" I whined. "I have no license to drive there now. This can't be right." I didn't know that I could drive in any state with the license I had.

Helen looked at me with the same Mona Lisa smile she always had and just said, "It's all going to be fine. Don't worry." Well, I worried and worried. But she was right.

I ended up taking the job and didn't need the Kansas license after all. I had a job, one that paid twice what I made in Kansas. But I had no place to live, and despite Helen's best intentions, we couldn't find an acceptable place.

So I started my job at Mercy Hospital in Centerville, Ohio, and I started a new life. Mercy was much like the other hospitals I had worked in. It was pretty laid back and open to everyone. It was, after all, the hospital for that community. I lived with Stephen and Helen for about six months as I looked for something I wanted and could afford. We grew very close as Helen, Stephen, and I drove all over the place when I was off duty. What fun we had exploring forests, parks, restaurants, etc.! Helen and I also had a great time shopping. Stephen dreaded when we came home with a gazillion boxes that he would have to tear up for the trash pickup once a week.

Our favorite story about Helen was when Stephen and I drove in a terrible snowstorm through some tough terrain. She had warned us about going that way in bad weather, but we went anyway because it was the shortest distance. Needless to say, she was right, and we almost didn't make it back. We both laugh when we remember her standing there with her hands on her hips, chiding us, "I told you two not to go that way. You just don't listen!"

I could hardly believe how different my life was, and I gradually came to see that it was much better. I was being paid more than I had ever earned anywhere else, though it was a relatively easy job. I wasn't alone anymore and was really enjoying my new family. Sally and Sam weren't happy, though, because they expected me to move to Texas to be closer to them. That's probably what I would have done sooner or later. Even so, they were happy for me. They were always the best!

Sadly, I had Helen to run around with for only about three years before she got lupus and cancer. It hurt so much to see her suffer and be so sick. She was the kindest person I had ever known, and in that short time, I had come to love her like a sister.

Stephen was beside himself with grief; Helen was his life. "Susan, what can I do? I don't know what to do for her," he said in tears one morning.

"Stephen, you can do a lot by just being with her as much as you can. Hold her hand, caress her arm, and, most of all, talk to her. She can hear you even if she can't talk. Talk to her about your life together—how you met, when you got married, your love for her. That's what you can do for Helen." That's exactly what he did, and no one could have done it better. Stephen was wonderful with Helen until the very end.

My new job was fun at first as I was quickly accepted by the nursing staff, who seemed eager for any learning they could get. It was an instructor's dream, but a dream turned into a nightmare as nurse after nurse came to my office and asked if she could talk to me in confidence. As I listened to horror story after horror story, I realized that these nurses had been victimized by some vicious physicians who took advantage of women who had very little assets or resources.

It wasn't all the docs, by any means. It was just three or four, but that's three or four too many.

Despite all I had lived through, I was still stunned by some of the things the women told me had been done to them. One of them, Kelly, a woman with curly dark hair and brown eyes sobbed as she tried to tell me about an affair she was wanting out of. "Susan, do you have any idea what it's like to have someone like Dr. Martin threaten you? It's damn scary, I'll tell you that. He's connected. He can do anything he wants in this community. He's got the police, the judges all in his back pocket. Oh God, I'll never get out of this mess until I'm dead," she cried.

I tried to reassure her. "Kelly, yes, you can. We have to find ways to get you in a more secure place, and then you have to just tell him you're done with the affair."

"Oh, Jesus, where would I go? I have to work!" "We'd get you in a shelter here."

"That won't work," Kelly sobbed. "He'll be waiting right out here for me."

"Okay," I said, "let's just talk right now about what has happened to you—get it out of your system. We'll work on solutions later."

Kelly described how he ended every encounter by telling her what he would do to her if she ever told anyone. Oh God, Kelly cried, I can't talk about it anymore. It doesn't matter— he's going to kill me sooner or later. I'm marked, doomed. And I don't know why I'm talking to you. Remember you promised not to tell anyone—anyone!"

"Yes, I did promise that and I will keep my promise. I give you my word," I said as I softly patted her arm. Good God, this is egregious, I thought. But what could I do? If I did anything, he'd know, and she'd be the ultimate victim—a dead one! So I became the resident counselor for nursing service. At least, I told myself, I can listen to them and offer ideas that might help. That's better than nothing. A couple of months later, when I arrived at work one morning, staff told me that our Chief Nursing Officer (CNO), Tom Beers, just left. I wasn't sure what that meant but quickly found out when our CEO, Josh Bland, called me to his office and told me he was appointing me Chief Nursing Officer! I was stunned but set about the task of informing nursing staff of this huge and sudden change.

I was surprised to see that the nursing staff for the most part were ecstatic about the change.

Guess you could say there was dancing in the halls. I knew I had my work cut out for me, but I loved a challenge. First and foremost, I had to bring the team together quickly. We began meeting as a team regularly to discuss issues and to air gripes. I was pushing the concept of "one for all and all for one," because we desperately needed the solidarity of a team to give us strength.

I was making my rounds early one morning when I heard one of the good-old-boy doctors berating one of the staff nurses. "My dog is smarter than you," he told her loudly enough that passing visitors and staff heard it.

"I—I'm sorry, Doctor," she stuttered. "I misread your order, but I caught it before it got to the patient."

"It's a good thing, too, or I'd have your job!" He turned to find me standing right there, quietly observing it all.

I said, "Well, Dr. Fang, if that's what happened when we all made mistakes, there wouldn't be any staff or doctors, now would there?"

Fang glared at me, puffing up like an adder. "You stay out of this. It's none of your business," he spat. And, literally, his spit hit my face.

"That's where you're wrong, doctor. Bullying the nursing staff is exactly my business, and while we're at it, stop spitting in my face."

I can tell you that that encounter made the rounds of that hospital so fast it was as if we had town criers on every unit. Unbeknownst to me, nurses and staff told the story over and over. They had a champion—finally.

The nursing team began to coalesce; we had parties, and we designed T-shirts with mottos that we developed ourselves. We began a new way of thinking that was all about the team. We protected each other by watching out for trouble and alerting the other members of the team. Nurses began to assert themselves to anyone who tried to bully them. If they weren't successful, I got the call. One day, I was called to a med-surg unit, where a doctor was ordering the staff to prepare to do a procedure on a female patient there on the unit—without anesthesia. It was indeed a minor procedure, but it was still invasive. The staff nurses were beside themselves, because their arguments didn't work with this physician.

I sat down at the nursing station desk where the doc was reviewing the patient's chart. "Dr. Cruel I want to discuss the procedure you're planning for this patient and why you aren't doing it in the OR, where it should be done."

"Oh, Susan, there's no need to tie up the Operating Room (OR) for a simple case like this. You know, a couple of snips, and I'll be done!"

"Well, Dr. Cruel, a couple of snips or not, I can't let you do it. It is wrong for the patient, and it violates your very own medical staff policy. I'd be happy to get a copy of it for you, in case you don't remember all of it."

That's when it went from bad to worse. He sneered at me and reached over and put his hand on my thigh. "Susan, don't you worry your little self about this. I've been doing it for years, and I know what's good for my patient"—big emphasis on the I.

I leaned toward him and whispered, "Take your hand off my leg, or I start screaming." His face registered my seriousness, and he jerked his hand off my leg. "Now," I said, "let me get the supervisor to schedule this case in the OR for you."

He was exasperated, but having no card left to play, he cooperated. Again, the story went all over the hospital in a nanosecond. Nursing had scored a big one, and I had solidified the team.

Of course, it wasn't always the doctors at fault. I dealt with several nurses and other staff who didn't conduct themselves appropriately either. One worker saw nothing wrong with sending text messages all around the hospital with pictures from her parties from the past weekend where various staff members were drunk and halfway naked! I had to counsel her and she was defensive – something about freedom of speech!

On a much more serious note is the case of a nursing assistant who did something so awful, I still get upset when I think about it. This guy, while caring for patients in our orthopedic unit on the night shift, was caught by the patient—a young, attractive, blond female—masturbating over her bed while she was asleep. I know, you can't make these things up. I was called right then to come in, which did. When I got to the patient unit, everyone was running around like chickens with their heads cut off.

"Okay, everyone, let's huddle," I said, which basically meant, let's see who's on first, who's on second, and so forth. Once I got everyone's attention, I got all the gory details. The patient was horrified and fearful for her life as she screamed for help. The first staff member in the room was an older RN, Mary Jo. "Mary Jo," I said, "what did you see when you went in the room, and how long did it take you to get there?"

"Well, I was in there in no more than a couple seconds. She didn't even finish the scream before I was in there, 'cause I was right across the hall, getting some fruit juice for another patient. I'll tell you, her scream scared me—almost peed on the floor. When I ran in there, first thing I saw was Scott, the nursing assistant, over in the corner, zipping up his pants, and Mrs. Morrison was crying and trying to talk at the same time. I couldn't really understand her, but she kept pointing at Scott. I just stayed with her until you got here, Susan."

"Good, where's Scott?"

"Oh, we called security, and they have him in the conference room."

I went in to see the patient first. One of the hardest things I've ever done—apologizing to a patient for allowing something so horrible happen to her while she was in our care. "Mrs. Morrison, I am Susan Masters, and I am the vice president of nursing services here at Mercy Hospital. I want to tell you how sorry I am that this happened to you.

I don't have the words to express how I feel. Can you tell me what happened?"

She went through her description of what happened to her again, and I listened closely. While she was speaking, her husband, Joe Morrison, arrived. I excused myself so they could be alone.

I charged through the conference room door, feeling like I wanted to tear this nursing assistant apart with my own two hands. How could he do something like this?! I got angrier by the moment, but I knew I had to calm down and control my feelings.

The first person I saw in the room was Scott's union rep, Charles Marshall, who was huddled with him. A security officer was there as well. "Somebody want to tell me what happened?" I snarled.

Bob, the security guy, jumped right in with his report. After his report, I asked Scott for his version of the events. Believe it or not, he blamed the patient, said she must have been dreaming and that she had actually flirted with him during the early evening. "'Susan, I'm not stupid. I wouldn't jeopardize my job doing something like that!

She was dreaming, and all I was doing was getting ready to get her vitals."

"While you were zipping up your pants? At two thirty in the morning? Was she having problems with her vitals?" I said with all the sarcasm I could muster.

At that moment, Charlie's voice boomed between us, "Susan, we need to take this up later. I have to talk to Scott, and let's set up a time to talk with him together tomorrow. We'll all be more rested then."

To make a long story short, that's what we did. After many meetings and testimonies, Scott lost his job. That was appropriate, but it didn't help Mrs. Morrison regain faith in health care professionals.

Then there was the day I was called to the OR. "Susan, you have to do something. Dr. Patterson is at it again. He threw an instrument during his last case and barely missed a tech. Of course, he's drunk."

"What did you do about it—his being drunk, I mean. Don't tell me you let him do surgery drunk!"

Julie, the OR supervisor, paled as she said, "I didn't know he was drunk until the case was almost done."

"Oh my, what does this staff need to do their job and prevent doctors from operating who shouldn't operate? We've given them the tools they need and the support they need to do their jobs and still—here we are!"

"Susan," Julie stammered, "I don't know what went wrong."

"Well, here's what we're going to do. You and I are going to see Dr. Patterson in his office. He has to be confronted about his behavior. Then we will have him go through fit testing for work. He isn't fit to work, and that process will help us do what needs to be done. Remember, it's our job to protect the patients and the staff from events like this."

After several confrontations with Dr. Patterson, I succeeded in getting him into a fitness-for-work evaluation. He ended up going to a physician's rehab facility. It was too bad, he had been a great surgeon.

But four years later, I heard a knock on my office door and looked up to see him standing there. He asked to speak to me and told me what had been going on in his life. I got up and walked toward him so our conversation would be easier. He told me that he was back working as a surgeon in another state, but was "home" for a week and had come to thank me for really saving his life, his career, and his family. I was speechless. He saw the surprise on my face, and with his usual big grin said, "The A A requires that we go back and thank people for what they did for us as well as apologize for what we did to them. So here I am to tell you both things. I'm sorry for the trouble I caused, and I am very thankful for the steps you took. You believed in me." He reached down and gave me a hug, and out the door he went. *Wow*, I thought, *who would have believed that?*

Now to the boardroom side of this story. Attending hospital board meetings was one of the really different responsibilities that came my way as a result of being vice president of nursing. This is where I learned what power and politics really mean. It was the good-old-boys' network all over again; four men who ran the whole thing. The decisions weren't made in the meetings but rather over drinks somewhere or in one of their homes—and sometimes even in the hospital hallways. Two of these guys were physicians, and they really ran the board. Everyone listened to them because they feared what would happen if they didn't and also because they carried an aura of authenticity because of being docs.

I watched my boss and how he interacted with the board chairperson and the board in general. I was surprised at how deferential he was to board members and especially the chairperson. He was always commenting, "I serve at the pleasure of the board," which left me feeling insecure.

One of the most exasperating learning experiences of my career occurred right about then. I was stunned to learn that the board members, most of whom knew nothing about health care or hospitals, had made the decisions about what should be done or not be done for the organization and for the patient. *How can that be?* I thought. I didn't realize it but I had a lot to learn. My main responsibility at those meetings was running various contracts for physicians or physician groups. Sounds easy, but it was anything but easy. It wasn't easy because the doctors on the board and several other board members had an intense dislike for physicians that "didn't fit," made "too much money," or just didn't join their circle. They worked behind the scenes to defeat motions that were proposed to increase the compensation of doctors who weren't part of the good-old-boys' club. This increased my workload tremendously. I had to research reasons for the increases to greater depths than ever before. *Fair market value* was a term I came to hate. Most of all, I was saddened to see good doctors fight with each other over greed and jealousy. Some things never change.

One of the most memorable points in my career started with a simple idea. It came to me as I drove to work one morning. I had been struggling with RN staffing for months. Despite my attempts to partner with several colleges and universities to help me staff the hospital with the necessary RNs, I was unable to make it happen. In 2002 we spent over $1.2 million dollars for agency RNs—that is, per diem nurses. These nurses were there today and gone tomorrow. Besides costing a lot, they were hard on morale, and our care suffered. Ergo, *the idea.*

We're a hospital, I thought. *And hospitals can open diploma RN programs.* Off to the races I went. Would you believe that everyone except my boss thought it was a bad idea. We can't afford it, you'll never get faculty, and on and on. My boss, nonclinical that he was, still got it. That was good. I pulled our preliminary data together, and we asked to appear before the Ohio State Board of Nursing (OSBN), which licensed all schools of nursing in the state. My boss and the board chairperson went with me.

I was pretty pumped, because this great idea of mine was really going to help the hospital. Imagine my shock when I got the tongue-lashing of my life. I was quickly informed that my idea would set the profession of nursing back fifty years. I didn't know I had that kind of power.

Some of the members of the OSBN around the table were furious with me for thinking of such an idea and found it hard to believe that I had tried everything else, like working with a university. Well, I had the documentation to prove that I had tried to work with not one but five universities—to no avail. None of their faculty was willing to come over the mountain. What few people understood was that the prospective students were unable to go to a four- year university. Many of them had no vehicle, no parents to help, and often were single parents themselves. They plain couldn't afford a university education unless it came to them. I understood this population; after all, I was one of them.

After the OSBN lectured me, they sent me away with a resounding no. We got in the car, and as we started toward home, our board chairperson said, "Well, I guess that's the end of that." But from the back seat he heard a little voice say, "We're not done yet."

And we weren't. I knew that the board could not just say no. They had to have a reason, and the reason had to be one of the criteria they had for schools of nursing. So I went back to every board meeting for several months and just sat outside their meeting room. They saw me every time they came out of their meetings; I know this because they glanced at me as they walked past. After a few months of this, the board chair stopped as she went by and looked at me. "You're not going to go away, are you?"

"No, ma'am. I'll be sitting right here until you give me a chance to talk about my program. My hospital needs this to survive, and I know we can do it and do it right."

I presented the program at the next meeting of the board, and although there was some strong opposition, the vote was in my favor. Why? Because they couldn't find a reason to deny me, and the burden to prove that was on them.

I was ecstatic. I began to work on the curriculum at home every weekend. There was a lot to do, but it was a labor of love. Fast-forward a few months, and the program opened with nine students. It was 2005, and I had no trouble getting qualified faculty; I just paid more than the programs in the area. I also attracted people who wanted to be a part of something new.

From that point on, we had all the RNs we needed and no agency nurses worked in our hospital. The nursing program ran in the deficit until we got federal funding, but it was a small deficit that was more than covered by not paying for agency nurses.

Then I found out that my simple idea was much more important than I realized. It was a Saturday morning, and I went out to the mailbox to get my Saturday newspaper. I was in my pj's and robe and hoped no one was out there. Well, so much for that, because I was no more out there than I heard a voice call out, "Are you Susan Masters?"

I wanted to run back in the house, because I thought it was a complaint. But, as they got closer, I saw the smiles on their faces and knew it wasn't about a complaint. I said, "Yes, I'm Susan Masters. How can I help you?"

Finally the man called out, "We just wanted to tell you how much the school of nursing has impacted our granddaughter. We are so happy she had this option. We appreciate what you've done for our community." They waved and continued on with their walk.

Wow, I thought. *This is a bigger deal than I thought!* It felt really good to know that I had made a difference in someone's life.

Over the next several years, everywhere I went, people talked about what the school meant to the students who went to it and to the community as a whole. I was touched by the great stories our graduates told us as well. We not only fixed a problem at the hospital, we also made a huge difference in our community. The graduates got well-paying jobs and contributed tax money to the community as well as spending money in the community at the grocery store, the mall, and so on.

I thought it would be impossible to top all this, but I didn't know the future. Our school was not only successful in graduating a good number of students, it also achieved some amazing records. First of all, we had a five-year history of a 100 percent National Council Licensure Examination pass rate on the first try. This was a record in the state and might have been nationally as well. (We were unable to access the national data.)

And then we were notified that our program had been selected as the best nursing program in the state. We were on cloud nine, for sure. We were not just the best diploma nursing program in the state, but the best of all the nursing programs. We had letters of congratulations from everywhere, including the board of nursing, which had once told us they didn't want us to open at all. Who would have guessed?

Reflecting back on the Boardroom, Board politics were fascinating to me because I observed more and more at each meeting. The board had a finance committee that I had to attend as well, and at times I had to present reports. This was the most feared committee. The stories about what happened to people in that committee were legendary. An officer of the board chaired it.

On one occasion, I had to present a report regarding our neurology group. I was in charge of their contract as well, and it was time to renew it. And the docs were insistent on a raise in their stipend. I already knew that the board chair and member of the finance committee did not like the senior member of this group. I did my homework on this one, because I knew I would face opposition— big-time. I had national research regarding the level of compensation neurologists were receiving at the time as well as state and local data. I had calculated the revenues that the neurology group brought to the table, revenues that certainly exceeded expenses. I also had the latest scores on the Press Ganey surveys of the neurologists, and all their scores were good to very good. I spent a lot of time researching as well as talking with the neurology group's senior partner about the major points we wanted to make.

It was time, and a big drum roll played in my mind as I began to address the topic. "I am reporting tonight on the XYZ Neurology contract. It will expire in sixty days, and we are here tonight to seek approval for its renewal. The one major change we are requesting is to increase the stipend to the neurologists. Please see attachment A for a detailed description of the requested change. Clearly—"

"You can't be serious," Dan, one of the board members, yelled, interrupting me. "Those guys make more money than just about anyone around here!" Dan had the floor, and he was in his glory. He ranted about the money we paid to this group and to others and insisted that we should just stop doing it, as if that were an option.

"Dan," I said, fighting to keep my voice under control, "maybe you should give me a chance to summarize this material before you overreact. And remember, if you or a loved one has a stroke, these are the guys you'll want to be there."

Well, I felt better having said that, but he didn't. "How dare you speak to me like that," he snarled.

"Dan, I mean no disrespect, but we have to do this. We cannot exist as a hospital without neurologists. People won't even come to our ED; they'll go to our competitors because they can provide the service they need. We don't want to be a hospital that doesn't even have neurologists, do we?"

Dan turned to me and sputtered that he and his wife together don't make that kind of money. Before I could stop myself, I smiled and said, "Maybe you should have been neurologists instead of insurance agents." There was a collective gasp, and I jumped in and announced that, barring any additional discussion, we were ready for the vote. I prevailed—twelve in favor and three opposed. Not bad, huh?

CHAPTER 8

CEO? ME?

I will never forget the day when my boss, Josh Bland, our CEO, left the hospital to attend a meeting in Columbus. A few hours later, I happened to look out the window to see him putting some things in his SUV and then drive off. I was puzzled by this, since he was supposed to be at that meeting. Nonetheless, I went back to my work.

My phone rang a few minutes later, and the board chairperson greeted me. "Susan, we need you to come over to the board room right now," he said.

"Oh," I said, feeling a little weird. "You mean right now?" "Yes, we are waiting for you," he added and hung up.

I felt like something ominous was happening but was clueless. So, what was there to do but to head up to the boardroom. When I got there and entered the room, all the officers of the board were there, looking at me. I was a little scared, and I was sure that something big was going down—like they were going to fire me. I look back on this moment and know I probably looked stupid just standing there, gawking at everyone, but I couldn't get a word out of my mouth.

After what seemed like an eternity, Tom, the current chairperson, said, "Susan, Josh is gone. We let him go, and now we want you to accept the position of interim CEO. We think you will make an excellent CEO, but we want to make the offer on an interim basis so we all have a chance to see how it works before we make a commitment." He smiled at me and asked the others if they had any comments.

Everyone was very positive and encouraging. I watched for those who may not be really on board with the idea but didn't notice any at all. "But what happened to Josh, and where is he?" I asked.

Tom came over to me and looked into my eyes. "Susan, we can't talk about Josh or what happened, but he's on the way home. Now we need you to think about the future and, most importantly, this hospital's future. We need you to step up to a very important challenge."

I thought a couple of minutes and stammered, "Okay, I'll do it." Truth be told, I wasn't sure I knew what to do. I stood there thinking, *I can't believe this. All those years ago, I started this journey, carrying bedpans and answering patients' call lights, and here I stand now in a boardroom, being asked to be their CEO. Well, it's like a Cinderella story, the American dream!* I snapped back to reality as everyone was congratulating me and offering their encouragement. *Wow! What a day this was*, I thought, even as I wondered how Josh was.

The next few days were a whirlwind of activity. People congratulated me, people started working on getting me to do what they wanted me to do, and there were well-wishers and some naysayers. It was a huge moment for me when I moved into Josh's office. I think that's when it became a reality for me. *I'm the president/chief executive officer! Susan Masters, RN, MS, CEO. Oh my God, can I even do it? Do I have the skills?* All these thoughts whirled around in my head in a cloud of confusion. I remembered how many times Josh had asked me what to do, and I always knew the answer or where to find it. *Truthfully, I have a ton of experience, I told myself, experience that will help me in this role tremendously.*

So began my tenure as the chief executive officer of Mercy Hospital. I got past the initial hubbub and centered in on my platform. I held many meetings, both internally with the staff and externally with the community, to articulate my platform, which was based on three things:

Transparency—I promised that I would share all information I was able to share. I knew secrecy would be counterproductive.

Open-door policy—My door was open. Staff could stop me in the hallways. I would rather deal with issues as they arose then to schedule meetings later.

Civility—Everyone was to treat everyone with respect at all times—no exceptions. (It's probably evident to you where my desire for civility came from. After my childhood and my first marriage, I was compelled to see to it that others didn't go down that pathway.)

I defined each of the three prongs of my platform and answered questions anyone had. I felt very comfortable in front of these people and actually enjoyed it a lot. We had some great discussions during those meetings, and it was the beginning of a relationship I would build over the next decade—a relationship that would serve us all well.

Yet not everyone was happy. A few of the doctors really were upset that a nurse was in the position of CEO. They thought a nurse belonged over there, not over here. This reaction surprised me. I expected their disagreement, but not that it would be about me being a nurse. I expected they would be upset because a woman had the position, but it took a different twist. "Nurses will drive this hospital into the ground," they screeched. These doctors were pillars of the community, powerful men who wanted life to continue as it had been. Then I started getting phone calls again— calls meant to scare or intimidate me. At least there were no kids involved.

While I was making rounds one day, Dr. Southard, a well-known internist stopped me at the nurse's desk, glared at me, and loudly said, "Nurses should be nurses, not CEOs!"

"Well," I said, "doctors should be doctors and take care of their patients instead of bossing nurses around." I turned on my heels and walked away. I heard some of my staff snickering, pleased that I had spoken up to the demagogue doctor, but I also knew I had made an enemy. Still, it felt good—really good—to stand up to that bully.

Nothing could match what happened at home not long after that. The threatening phone calls had intensified and were occurring at night—just like before. When I answered the phone, I heard a low, muffled voice telling me what someone was going to do to me if I didn't quit and let some guy who was qualified have the job. With each call, this man got more and more specific and dramatic. Finally, when I heard his voice, I just hung up. But in my position, I had to answer the phone. I even got notes telling me how ugly I was and newspaper clippings with my picture all crossed out!

One peaceful Saturday morning, I opened my front door to go get the newspaper, and there on my doorstep lay a cat. I looked down at it, wondering why it didn't move. My brain finally recognized that it was dead. *Yikes*, I thought, how did a cat die right on my doorstep, and whose cat is it? I leaned down to look for a nametag, and that's when I saw that the cat's throat had been slit.

I started to gag and retch before I could control myself. I couldn't get my mind around the fact that someone would do something like that. Dear Lord, I thought, protect me and all of us from this madman. I knew that I had to get the police involved, even though I hated to for a lot of reasons, including the impact on the hospital and my prior experiences with situations like this. But I called them, and I was pleasantly surprised. The cop who responded got a detective into the picture right away. They were both very supportive, and I never got the sense that they didn't believe me or thought I was a "silly woman." That was such a change from my experiences in Kansas, but that had been more than twenty years before, too.

I went back to work on Monday and tried to pretend nothing was wrong, but I found myself wondering who it was. I listened to each doctor's voice carefully to see if he was the one. It wasn't even a week, though, before the police called and told me that they caught the guy, and he even confessed that a local doctor had paid him to "scare me." But he wouldn't give anyone the name of that doctor.

I was relieved and stunned at the same time. *Are you kidding me*, I thought. *A doctor actually paid this guy to do these things. A doctor? For God's sake, I've worked with doctors all my life; we're on the same team! What did I do wrong or what did I fail to do?* I started to I mull over this whole thing, but then I jerked my head up and told myself, *Do not think like that. That's your Irish Catholicism talking. You did nothing wrong.* I had to repeat that two or three times to get myself away from that kind of thinking.

The guy ended up going to prison and was killed in brawl there. I know because the detective on my case kept checking, hoping that he would tell us who paid him. So we'll never know.

Back to the everyday world, the first, most important task I took on as the new CEO was to reorganize our board of directors. What I had inherited was not going to work going forward. Openings presented themselves, because an effort to get rid of me polarized the board. Utilizing my best skill, which I call 'quiet calmness', I planned strategies and executed moves until I had the chessboard the way I wanted it. I had neutralized the opposition and stacked the board with "friendlies."

In addition, I nominated the local Catholic priest to our board, along with a female college professor with a PhD and some physician friends who knew and agreed with my platform. They all won seats on the board.

When the next Board Chair was elected, it turned out to be a real blessing to me and to the organization. It was a stroke of good fortune that a man with his skill set turned up at the right moment in time.

Scott Harriston had been a board member for years and had only a couple more years to serve. He was so concerned about the future of the hospital that he felt he should step up. So step up he did; he volunteered to be the next chairperson—not a duty he wanted at that point in his life, but a duty he accepted because someone had to.

I don't know if he had any idea what would happen during his tenure. If he had, he might have run the other way. No, he wouldn't have run at all—not Scott! It was the time when debts had to be paid. All the credit for what happened next goes to him. Scott was in his seventies, in excellent health, and a man who presented himself well: tall, ramrod straight with gray hair and sky-blue eyes. And he wasn't your run-of-the-mill board member. He was highly experienced in management and human resources, and he knew how to handle almost any situation. Most of all, he was a no-nonsense person. He would tell you what you needed to hear, not what you wanted to hear, in a very direct manner. You understood Scott when he talked to you. Yet he was warm and caring. His directness is an attribute that all managers should have. It saves time and stress for all parties.

As we sat in my office a couple of months after he took office, he looked at me eye to eye and began describing the problem we had. He got my attention immediately when he said, "Look, Susan, I've done your annual evaluation here, and we're going over it first." I didn't even know he had done it, so my blood pressure was up for sure.

In retrospect, Scott did an awesome job with that evaluation. I didn't think so then, of course. In short, I learned that while I was doing a decent job, many of the board members felt that there was too much contention between some of the members of the board and me, particularly the physician members. They also indicated that I was at times curt and almost disrespectful to them. This criticism really wounded me. I felt like a martyr. *After all the horrible things I've been through—the murdered cat, the awful phone calls—and this is what I get?*

But the next thing Scott did left me feeling totally different. He put down all his papers and leaned toward me. "Susan, you're the best CEO this hospital has ever had; you just have to smooth out some relationships that you've damaged. You can do that in your sleep if you put your mind to it." His words were soft, and his expression was kind and hopeful. I suddenly felt like everything was going to be fine. I understood now, and I could do exactly what Scott said I could do.

We talked for a couple of hours about everything, and out of that came a plan that I wanted to follow. I shared it with Scott, of course, and he agreed with it completely. So, at the next board meeting, I read a prepared statement under my report to the board. In that statement, I apologized to the board for my behavior and thanked them for their candid review of my performance that opened my eyes to what I was doing without realizing it.

Scott finished with his report, wherein he told the board how he felt about my work overall. "I've been involved with the board for twenty years. This is the best

CEO we've ever had. She needed some feedback, and we gave it to her. Now you have heard what her plan is, and I think all of you will agree with it. This is the first time we've had a leader who isn't afraid to lift up a rock to see what's under it. Not only does she do that, but if there's a snake under the rock, she kills it!" And just like that, Scott and I and rest of the board became a team.

The next memorable hurdle was when the executive committee of the board (the board officers) gave me an assignment that would bring me more trouble with the docs. They wanted me to reverse the financial damage in our physician group. They gave me thirty days to formulate a plan, which I was to bring back to them before implementing it.

I formulated a plan, conferred with the board officers, and executed the plan. It included firing the manager, Stan, and eliminating providers who weren't pulling their own weight. We had all the information in our database. So, armed with the data, I called Stan in for a discussion. The conversation went badly. Stan was a bit of an egotist; he was an "I walk on water" kind of guy. So, to hear me, this little nurse, tell him he not only wasn't perfect but was indeed flawed did not go over well. In fact, he leaned toward me until he was just about in my air space, scowling in a threatening kind of way, saying, "Nurses are going to be the end of this hospital," a common phrase around the hospital those days. Then he stomped out of the room. I breathed a sigh of relief, because I thought he was going to hit me. I should have had someone with me. Lesson learned!

Next I called in the physicians who were far below their productivity targets, and of those, only the ones who represented specialties that we could still cover or that someone in the community covered. I didn't want to leave anyone in the community without medical coverage. This sole action hit the medical community in my little town like a tsunami. It had not been done before at our place, and boy, did people react. The reactions were mixed but most of them were in defense of the doctors and how the big, bad hospital had treated them.

The worst situation, hands down, came when I had to tell another doctor, one of my personal friends, Dr. Jeff Johnson, that his contract was being terminated, too. Knowing him well made what I had to tell him really suck!

I'll digress a moment to an incident that happened a few years before. This doc, Jeff Johnson, and I already were good friends. It all began when I traveled with him to New York City for a weeklong conference when I was the vice president of nursing. I got to know him really well because we were together day and night. I knew he was a real jokester, so I would tell him, "While we're in the session, don't make me laugh." Of course, he did everything he could to do so.

What endeared me to him was how he treated me: I was the lady, and he always treated me that way, even when others were around. He held the door for me and looked out for me. That touched me, because I seldom experienced it with other docs. His love for his family impressed me so deeply. I heard him call them a couple of times every day and I heard how he talked to them. He told me all about his life and I felt close to him because our values were the same.

That night in Manhattan, the CEO, Josh, and his wife were going to take us to a very prestigious restaurant, where we were meeting a couple who were friends of theirs. We were all dressed to the nines—it was Manhattan, after all. We were waiting to meet Josh's friends when two people ambled up to him. On first glance, I thought they were theater people. She was wearing a dress that looked like it came from the forties, long white gloves that went all the way up her arms, and finally, *le pièce de rèsistance*, a hat that had long feathers covering most of her face. In fact, I couldn't see her face at all. And she never took it off nor did she remove her gloves. Now, my mother taught me better than that.

Her husband, Mr. Oscar, was wearing a black tuxedo complete with a top hat and—yes, I'm serious—a cape. When did you see anything like that in person? Turns out that this odd couple weren't actors at all but Josh's friends. So, off to dinner we went in that upscale restaurant in Manhattan that Josh loved and that had only about fifteen tables—small ones at that. We were getting to know each other a little as we chatted over cocktails. They were both physicians from Upstate New York—he was a urologist and she was in family medicine.

Everyone was chatting about their own worlds when Jeff started to describe a patient experience he had that he should have kept to himself. He was seated to my right, the New Yorkers were directly across from me, and my boss and his wife were to my left. Without even looking up from his food, Jeff said, "Boy, it's tough out there.

Some of these patients I see are unbelievable. I mean, I was examining this gal the other day, and damn if she didn't have lice all over her pubis and—"

The shriek of the urologist interrupted him. "My God, man, don't say things like that at the dinner table." He was waving his arms and, of course, the cape, too. At the same time, Josh spewed a mouthful of his martini right straight across the table while his wife, Stephanie, was bent over with laughter. Mrs. Urologist was motionless; with those feathers over her eyes, I wasn't sure she was even conscious.

Jeff looked at me and said, "Geez, you wouldn't think he'd get upset over what I said. He's a urologist, for Christ's sake." You had to give it to him!

Well, after that remarkable event, things were a little strained between Jeff and Mr. and Mrs. Urology. We finished our dinner and prepared to leave. Josh's two friends walked out just ahead of us while Josh and his wife headed out in another direction. None of us knew that another unfortunate incident was lurking in the shadows!

It was dark and Jeff and I were walking behind Mr. and Mrs. Urology to return to our hotel when I tripped over something I didn't see and began to fall. The only option I had to prevent myself from God knows what kind of injury was – you guessed it – the cape! I grabbed that cape and held on for dear life while, in the process, Mr. Urology was almost choked to death as I pulled on the back from behind him and it tightened around his throat. I kept myself from falling but the poor doc was all bent over, sputtering and coughing like the end was near.

'Urology clearly wanted to bonk me one. Jeff, on the other hand, was only worried about me. What a doll! The next thing I knew, everyone was gone, and it was just Jeff and me. So the two of us went to a bar, got a couple drinks, and laughed ourselves silly over what we called the 'cape escapade'.

Back to what I was talking about in the first place: the restructuring of our physician group. To make a long story short, I got the job done, and in about a year we began to see positive effects. Looking back now, I can see that it was the right, though painful, thing to do. Because we did it with as much caring and sensitivity as possible, it worked. We were civil, transparent (as much as we could be), and caring through it all, even when met with anger.

Our board meetings remained my major focus. I had to be prepared for anything to happen and have a response ready. Saying something like "I'll find the answer and get back to you" can be used only occasionally. The CEO is expected to know the answers. Questions were often hostile and intended to trip me up or to cause me to lose control— or God forbid, cry. I can tell you that I would have died before I cried in front of those people.

There were some particularly valuable tools that I did use successfully:

- Smile. It portrays a positive and capable attitude and throws the enemy off. Smile even when you're going to say something that will be perceived as negative. I learned this technique from a psychiatrist friend.
- Stay calm. It never helps to lose control, and it rattles the enemy's confidence the most.

- Ask for specifics. Whenever the other person is citing something "horrible" that you're responsible for, ask for specific details so you can look into the problem. He or she almost never has the specifics, and you're off the hook.
- Apologize when indicated. This shouldn't occur often; if it does, you probably don't belong in the job.

Early on in my career as a CEO, it wasn't unusual for fights to break out at board meetings. I'll always remember the one that broke out over a very contentious issue surrounding our hospitalist program. I was running the contract for the program, a contract we had with another system that provided 24/7 hospitalist coverage for a hospital, something we couldn't do on our own because we didn't have the doctors. Our family medicine docs no longer wanted to practice inpatient medicine, which was the real reason that drove us to using a hospitalist program. While some of my board members understood, some did not.

What we were experiencing was happening all over the country. It was actually the evolution of American medicine into a new reality that brought much angst to small community hospitals without the resources or capital to resolve issues like this one. Everybody, including the board members who had people in the community complaining to them every day, wanted their own personal physician to treat them like they had for many years, and for good reason. I told them that the old-time doc who would always be there was gone. They were replaced with docs who were very interested in their patients but who were not willing to be available 24/7. Ergo, we had a contract with a hospitalist group that would see everyone's patients while they were in the hospital—except for those doctors who still wanted to see their own patients.

This is the reason for the fistfight that ensued at one of our board meetings. I had presented data to the board about the dollar impact of the hospitalist contract—data that showed an increase in fees paid to these docs. The fees were still within the accepted range but sent one of our board members over the edge. This was a guy by the name of Jack Johnson, a local businessman who was well known for his mouth. Under it all, he was anti-physician.

He started his usual anti-doc rhetoric when the president of our medical-dental staff, a member of the board and a champion of physician interests, Charles Calley, interrupted him. "Johnson, you just hate it when docs get raises and make more money than you do or that the majority of the people in this community make! Well, it's a reality you better get used to if you want a hospital." He banged the desk with his fist, sputtering something about the educational level of the community in general and the board specifically.

The comment about the educational level pushed all the buttons for Johnson, who jumped from his chair and ran toward Calley, brandishing his fist. "How dare you talk about my community like that. You're an outsider anyway!" "Well, I guess thirty years don't count, huh? I'm an outsider after practicing here for over thirty years," Calley said as he rose from his chair. Johnson threw a punch at Calley, who ducked in the nick of time and returned a blow that landed right between Johnson's eyes.

"Oh my God, should we call security?" I yelled to my board chairperson.

"Call them now before this turns into a complete fiasco," he said. Then he jumped up and pounded his gavel so hard I looked to see if he broke it. He yelled, "Charlie and Jack, sit down, both of you! If you can't control yourselves, security is on the way, and they'll escort you to your cars."

Just as security came through the doors to our meeting room, both of the men sat down at their seats, and the board chairperson regained control. We had security remain for the rest of the meeting, which turned out to be no problem. The motion to approve the new contract for the hospitalist program was approved with two dissenting votes and thirteen affirmative. Another battle won! Of course, there was a lot of banter between the antagonists as we finished our meeting, but at least they stayed in their seats.

I was pretty sure Johnson was going to have a black eye from the punch he took, but, hey, not my doing.

So, the years passed and I still had the reins when the board, led by its new not our community hospital should join a large system. This turned out to be a watershed event. Nothing was the same after that moment. We appointed a subcommittee of the board to do the yeoman's work regarding mergers. We hired a consultant, who charged us an obscene amount of money to—you know—tell us what we already knew. Still, that was necessary to be sure we addressed all the legal issues that surround mergers. They did that well.

For the first several months, our subcommittee reviewed reams of data about various mergers, listened to our legal counsel's summary of such matters, and argued among them about what form was best for us. One of our board and subcommittee members was actually involved in a merger of his own business there in town. His experiences were helpful, but we needed strength and confidence.

While the subcommittee had very different opinions about what should be done, they were united in their mission. Most of all, though, all of them told me that they supported me 100 percent, which was great to hear but scary at the same time. Change is hard—even positive change.

So, there we were, at that watershed meeting wherein the vote would be cast that would set the direction for the hospital and community for the foreseeable future. But wait! That's where this story began.

CHAPTER 9

THE LEGACY

I sat back in my chair, watching this remarkable family celebrate the arrival of a new member, Susan's great granddaughter—four generations of women! I looked over at her, sitting back in her chair like the old grand dame in European literature, reflecting on our lives, enjoying the moment. As I looked around the room, my heart filled with warmth. Susan's son, Sam, and his wife, Martha, are arm in arm. Her grandson, Seamus, is hugging them both. Her dear daughter, Sally, and her daughter, Kathy, are absorbed with the new life in front of them: our new baby girl.

I am so thrilled that I was able to be a part of this remarkable woman's life and family. Often I was far away but I have been a part of their lives and a part of her heart for over forty years. We were never married, Susan and I, but we always felt each other's touch. Chicky, I thought, you're the love of my life, a thought that brought a smile to my heart.

There she sits, straight as an arrow with the same smile as always and those same dark eyes—the almond shape, the almost-black pupils, black as black can be with sparks that remind you of electrical storms. Sally has the same color eyes and the almond shape. But Kathy shares the flash-and-flicker trait. Now here is this new baby, and her eyes are shaped the same. The family trait continues! Will the most telling trait of this great family continue on in this baby? Time will tell. I must let things play out as they should.

Susan's son, Sam, who carries the genes of her father, smiles warmly as he takes in the emotions of the moment then says, "Mom, you are the anchor of this family—a great family with all the tribulations and triumphs of ten families. You know, we don't talk about these things very often, but we should. It's important to tell our story over and over so that all of us know it by heart and so that others hear it, too. Our family is built on endurance and hope— you have ensured that. We, your children, grandchildren, and now great-grandchild, salute you and thank you for that. A toast everyone—to our mother, grandmother, and great-grandmother!"

How can a story end any better than this? I stand to join the toast to this family, whose lives I've shared. Yet it's a bittersweet moment. Deep inside, I know it's time. I know Susan's mortality is betraying her, impaling her. Her days on this earth are numbered. I feel it. Yet here is her great- granddaughter who, by her very breath, brings new life into this family. As I watch her, I realize that this family will always endure.

No one noticed as I quietly turned on the music, and the familiar refrain of "Rock Around the Clock" echoed softly through the room. "Chicky, let's do it one more time," I said, as I took her hand and began the steps we'd done so many times before, maybe a wee bit slower and maybe not so many flashy moves. "One, two, three o'clock, four o'clock, rock"—our signature song. I drew her close to me and lightly stroked her face as I always did, as we moved to the beat of our song. We were one again and once more.

When the music ended, everyone clapped for this couple who had survived so many obstacles and whose love had finally become their reality.

Amid the laughter of the family, bright with hope and triumph, holding their future, their circle enlarged now by one, Susan's voice speaks from the shadows with great solemnity and passion. "We're not done yet," she said, with her black eyes sparkling. "We're not done yet at all!" Suddenly, everyone clapped again in tribute to this family and how it all began so many years ago.

Here, at the end, you might ask, What next? Well, that answer is right before your eyes, telling a story so that others can benefit from it—the most extraordinary story I've ever heard. And I lived it along with her. She is the American dream.

Where else in the world could a little runt of a kid, so disadvantaged, wind up the CEO of a hospital? It's proof that miracles do happen! She would say she wasn't brilliant or extremely talented. Nor was she beautiful or rich. So, what is the ingredient that made this miracle happen?

Well, the answer to that question is the purpose of this story: to make you laugh and cry, maybe even at the same time, but most of all, to inspire you with the spirit to hold to dreams no matter what, to recognize that perseverance is more than half the battle. Indeed, the moral of this story is "Always have hope and never give up!" Oh, and keep dancing!